I WISH I READ
THIS BOOK BEFORE
MEDICAL SCHOOL

This book was conceived, designed, and produced by The Bright Press, an imprint of the Quarto Group, The Old Brewery, 6 Blundell Street, London N7 9BH, United Kingdom. T (0)20 7700 6700
www.QuartoKnows.com

All inquiries should be addressed to:
Peterson's Publishing, LLC
4380 S. Syracuse Street, Suite 200
Denver, CO 80237 -2624
www.petersonsbooks.com

ISBN 978-0-7689-4562-1

The Bright Press
Publisher: James Evans
Editorial Director: Isheeta Mustafi
Art Director: James Lawrence
Managing Editor: Jacqui Sayers
Development Editor: Abbie Sharman
Editor: Anna Southgate
Design: Lindsey Johns
Cover design: Grade

Printed and bound in China

9 8 7 6 5 4 3 2 1

FSC
MIX
Paper from responsible sources
FSC® C016973
www.fsc.org

I WISH I READ THIS BOOK BEFORE MEDICAL SCHOOL

ADVICE ON HOW TO ADJUST, SUCCEED, AND THRIVE AT MEDICAL SCHOOL

DR. KATHERINE CHRETIEN

ABOUT THE AUTHOR

DR. KATHERINE CHRETIEN

Dr. Katherine Chretien is associate dean for student affairs and medical student wellness at Johns Hopkins School of Medicine. Previously, she was associate dean for student affairs and professor of medicine at George Washington University School of Medicine and Health Sciences. She earned her undergraduate degree in Neuroscience from Brown University and attended the Johns Hopkins School of Medicine, graduating with Alpha Omega Alpha honors. She completed her internal medicine training at the Johns Hopkins Hospital. Dr. Chretien is the recipient of the Women Leaders in Medicine Award from the American Medical Student Association and the Charles H. Griffith III Educational Research Award from Clerkship Directors in Internal Medicine. Dr. Chretien has published her research and writing in the *Journal of the American Medical Association*, *Annals of Internal Medicine*, *Medical Education*, and *USA TODAY*. She was editor of the book *Mothers in Medicine: Career, Practice, and Life Lessons Learned* (Springer 2018). She married her medical school classmate, Jean-Paul, and has three children.

CONTENTS

INTRODUCTION

+

If you are reading this book, you are probably a soon-to-be or current medical student. Congratulations! As you know, getting accepted into any medical school is a feat that requires a ton of focus, grit, resilience, and hard work. I mean, organic chemistry alone. Major props to you. You are on the path to becoming a physician, with the incredible privilege of caring for the sick and maintaining people's health and well-being.

It may come as no surprise to you that attending medical school requires the same determination. In addition, it will require you to place continued (or renewed) focus on your own well-being. Prioritizing your well-being will improve your learning, deepen your resilience, and allow you to face what challenges await you. This is not always appreciated by medical students—when faced with the decision of whether to study 30 more minutes after a full day of studying or to go out for a run or walk, some students push on through, believing that that little bit of extra time will make a difference in their exam scores. They sacrifice their well-being in the process, and yet research shows that breaks and exercise improve focus and learning. You can make your learning the most efficient and effective possible by incorporating evidence-based learning and lifestyle strategies. That's just one of the topics covered in this book.

Primarily, this book is here to help you navigate medical school, with advice and tips to help you not just survive medical school, but to thrive there. Not every student can graduate with honors or be at the top of the class, but every student has the potential to develop the core competencies expected of a graduating medical student and successfully develop both professionally and personally during the process—and enjoy the journey! This book won't cover every single issue you might encounter or have questions about, but it aims to consider the main ones and those less likely to be completely covered by your medical school. All of us who attended medical school wish we could go back and give our younger selves some tips and hints to make our experience even richer and our time better spent. After writing this book, I honestly wish I, myself, had read it before medical school!

The chapters that follow discuss everything from the first days of medical school and getting organized to effective learning strategies and thriving on clinical rotations. They also offer advice on maintaining your well-being and your relationships, and many other things besides. They are informed by research, faculty, and dean colleagues, current and past students, and my experience as a student affairs dean responsible for advising students throughout their four years (and sometimes more) of medical school. This is not your mother's *Tips for Medical School* book— it includes contemporary topics such as virtual learning best practices, responding to microaggressions and discrimination, and navigating social media as a medical student. It will hopefully help you maintain perspective and be a guide for you during this formative time.

Every medical student has the potential to thrive.

Let's do this!

ABOUT THIS BOOK

This book is divided into several parts, and you can either start from the beginning and go straight through (recommended if just starting your medical school journey) or skip around based on your current needs as you are progressing through.

Throughout the book you will find quotes from faculty and students with their key advice, as well as longer selections from students and residents on topics where proximate experience matters. Look for these "Top Tips" scattered throughout the chapters.

PART I includes chapters entitled The First Days of Medical School and Finances and Budgeting, which aim to set you up to start medical school on the right foot. They cover the basics of getting yourself organized, oriented, and ready for learning. Don't skip this section if you are well into medical school, since some of these topics—growth mindset, impostor syndrome, and common pitfalls—are critical and evergreen.

PART 2 includes some essential topics concerning learning in the preclinical years that you will continue to use throughout school, including key learning strategies and approaches to studying and lifestyle habits that promote learning, contributing to teams, extracurriculars, summers and breaks, and research.

PART 3 focuses on well-being and relationships and may be consulted at any time. Chapters here look at finding mentors and being a mentee, well-being, resilience, and relationships in medical school.

PART 4 moves into choosing a specialty and clinical rotations. Read the chapter Choosing a Specialty early on in medical school and revisit as you move into clinical rotations.

PART 5 covers professional identity and diversity, equity, and inclusion. These are important topics for every student throughout medical school, so read these early and revisit as needed.

At the end of the book, you'll find Resources, with some templates for you to use or modify, as well as Further Reading, with a recommended bibliography for additional publications on some of the subjects covered.

PART

PREPARING FOR AND ARRIVING AT MEDICAL SCHOOL

CHAPTER ONE

THE FIRST DAYS OF MEDICAL SCHOOL

The first days of medical school are often filled with excitement, nervousness, and a whole lot of newness. From orientation to your first classes and the first exam, this is a transition period full of adaptation, trying new things, and establishing routines.

It can feel overwhelming when you first start. You may be new to the area and figuring out where to get groceries while trying to make friends and deciding what outside learning resources you may want to use. Know that things will settle with time and that your feelings are entirely normal. All transition periods are somewhat awkward and push us out of our comfort zones. Remember that it's when we're outside of our comfort zones that most growth happens. Embrace chaos and "fun fact" ice breakers!

This chapter covers some basic topics to help you start on the right foot and prepare for the tsunami of learning to come: orientation basics, getting yourself organized, dealing with impostor syndrome, and key qualities and mindsets for success, as well as common pitfalls to avoid. You may want to revisit parts of this chapter later on, once you're past the first days of medical school, if impostor syndrome creeps back in again or you find yourself feeling overwhelmed.

In the meantime, get ready for your first days.

ORIENTATION

It's finally here: medical school orientation. Over the next few days, you are going to meet a ton of classmates; be introduced to countless deans, faculty, and staff whose names you will promptly forget; and quite possibly suffer from information overload. You will likely engage in activities to help you get to know and bond with your classmates. You will also take care of lots of administrative tasks. Enjoy this time— it's the start to your medical school journey.

WHAT TO EXPECT

TIME TO MEET YOUR NEW CLASSMATES

Orientation includes time to start getting to know your new classmates. Some may eventually become close friends, rocks, possibly even life partners (no pressure!). Importantly, these are people you will be spending time with for the next four years.

TEAM-BUILDING ACTIVITIES

You will be working in teams throughout medical school and your career in medicine. Many schools run team-building activities from the first days to help you develop these skills. See Chapter Four: Contributing to Teams.

INTRODUCTION TO THE CURRICULUM

You will be given an overview of the curriculum and ways to approach studying.

ADMIN

There will be many administrative tasks to get everyone up and running—everything from taking your school photo, to IDs, IT setup, immunization records, and so on.

SPEAKERS, SPEAKERS, AND MORE SPEAKERS

You will likely hear from many people who will introduce you to resources, offices, and programs.

ORGANIZATION FAIR

Either during orientation or soon afterward, there is usually an introduction to all of the different student organizations you can participate in.

Pro tips

MAKING FRIENDS

It may take a while to meet your future closest friends in medical school. Don't expect to find your friendship group on the first day. Relax and just enjoy meeting everyone. It will come in time.

WHO'S WHO?

You'll be meeting and interacting with a lot of faculty members and administrative staff over your years of medical school. Here's a general guide to who's who.

 THE DEAN:
The dean is the highest executive of the medical school. They may even be the CEO of an associated teaching hospital.

 VICE DEAN/SENIOR ASSOCIATE DEAN:
This is the next level under the dean. They are responsible for large areas such as education or research.

ASSOCIATE AND ASSISTANT DEANS:
Other deans will lead specific areas, such as admissions, curriculum, or student affairs. Together, all the deans make up the administration.

DEPARTMENT CHAIRS:
Leaders of basic science (e.g., anatomy) or clinical departments (e.g., psychiatry) within the school.

COURSE OR CLERKSHIP DIRECTORS:
These are faculty members who run courses or clinical clerkships.

FACULTY:
All of the people who will teach and mentor you. Practicing physician faculty members are also called attending physicians.

Key to academic ranks

In academic medicine, faculty titles have a hierarchy.

Professors: Faculty members who have national or international recognition for their work in research, teaching, and/or service. These are referred to as "full professors."

Associate professors: Members who have earned recognition for their work in research, teaching, and/or service, but not to professor level.

Assistant professors: Members with local recognition for their work in research, teaching, and/or service.

Instructors: Often new members of medical school staff; they may be recently out of training.

ORIENTATION: RESOURCES

Your medical school will have many resources available to support you throughout your years. These resources can be hugely helpful to you, so it is important to have this information readily available for future use. Find somewhere handy to tuck it away.

ADVISORS

Who are those in the school who will serve as advisors to you? How will you set up meetings with them and how often? These are the people whose job it is to support you and your development. Get to know them early on.

ACADEMIC SUPPORT

You may have faculty members who can provide academic support when you are having difficulty. You could also use these people as a resource to maximize your study skills at any level of performance. Who is available and how can you access this support? Does your school have a tutoring program? Who are the tutors and how can you get set up with one?

STUDENT HEALTH

Medical school is not a time to neglect your health. Where is the student health service located? What are the hours, and how can you make an appointment? What is your insurance coverage? What should you do if you have a medical emergency?

WELLNESS

There will be a wealth of resources to support your wellness, including mental health support, wellness programs, and possibly entire offices devoted to student well-being. Find out what resources are available and note any that you may want to tap into.

Pro tips

ACADEMIC SUPPORT SERVICES

Many schools offer academic support services to help students maximize their learning. These services typically include:

+ Learning and study skills

+ Remediation

+ Peer tutoring

+ Time management

+ Organizational strategies

+ Medical licensing board preparation

+ Exam accommodations

MAXIMIZING ORIENTATION

Second-year medical student Meera Krishnamoorthy offers guidance on getting the most out of medical school orientation. Her advice relates primarily to traditional, in-person orientation, but many principles apply for virtual versions as well.

❶ Be open

Be vulnerable with others, open up, and be open to making connections with new people whenever you meet them. Try to put yourself out there and initiate hanging out after scheduled orientation events to get to know people better.

❷ Stay balanced

Don't let yourself get fatigued or overwhelmed by the volume of social activities; it's all about balance. If you need to take time to recharge by yourself, don't be afraid to do so.

❸ Keep fears in check

Take rumors about medical school that you hear from other incoming students with a grain of salt. Sometimes, students talk about stories they have heard, which can lead to them scaring each other before school has even started. Acknowledge your fears, but make sure they don't get in the way of you being able to appreciate the wonderful experience that is starting this new chapter in your life.

❹ Get organized

Make a Google Doc or spreadsheet specifically for resources that are shared. You can even make it collaborative with classmates if you want to. Use a calendar app to keep track of, or organize, events and schedule your days, and use a reminders app or to-do list to make sure you're accomplishing tasks on time.

STAYING ORGANIZED

Staying organized is essential for medical school. Even if you used a system before medical school that worked well, it could be beneficial to explore new or additional tools to keep on top of all of your to-dos; to balance the demands of a challenging curriculum, extracurricular activities, and research; or to organize your personal time and other pursuits. Whether you use a physical daily planner, purely digital tools, or a combination, find a system that works for you. Here are some ideas that may help you to stay on top of your organization and time-management game.

CALENDAR

This is essential for day-to-day and longer-term planning. What kind you use is up to you. Consider the email/calendar system your school uses but don't feel bound by it if it doesn't work for you. Don't forget to schedule in personal time. Use the different views—daily, weekly, monthly—to help you preview, plan, and view the big picture of what's ahead.

TO-DO LISTS

To-do lists will be your friends throughout medical school and residency (and perhaps the rest of your life). Set realistic, achievable goals. Marking off items can be immensely gratifying. It's okay if you haven't accomplished everything on your list by the end of the day. But do periodically assess to make sure you've completed the highest priority tasks each day. Explore apps that interface with your calendar, sync to your multiple devices, and/or use location-based reminders.

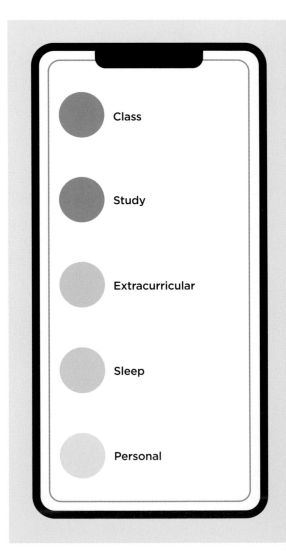

- Class
- Study
- Extracurricular
- Sleep
- Personal

TIME-MANAGEMENT AND PRODUCTIVITY HACKS

Need other tools to help you manage your time and keep you on schedule and focused when you need to be? There's an app for that. Some apps turn off your phone during set periods so you won't be distracted. Others help you track time spent or project progress. Share best-practice strategies with peers and develop organizational and time-management prowess.

Although the amount of time you spend on each activity will vary from student to student and school to school, make sure you are dividing your time well and stick to it.

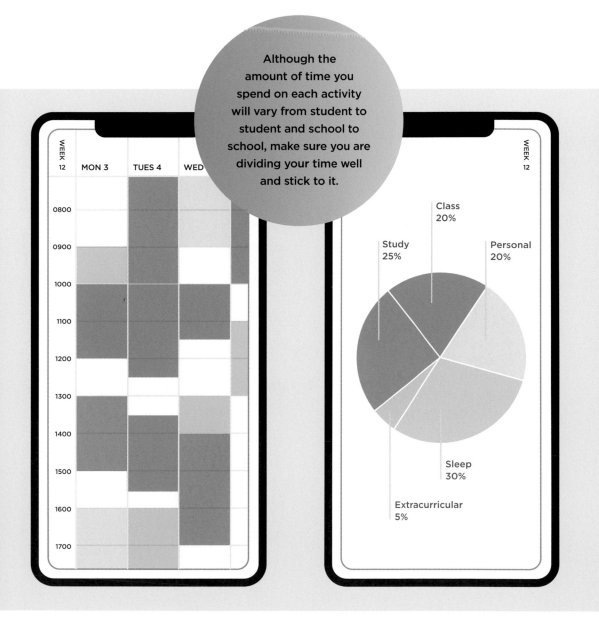

WEEK 12

	MON 3	TUES 4	WED
0800			
0900			
1000			
1100			
1200			
1300			
1400			
1500			
1600			
1700			

WEEK 12

Class 20%

Study 25%

Personal 20%

Sleep 30%

Extracurricular 5%

MANAGING YOUR INBOX

You thought you received a lot of email messages prior to attending medical school, but with the influx of messages from your professors, educational coordinators, student organizations, and the like, you may find it hard to keep up with important messages that contain critical due dates. Now is a good time to start a system to organize your emails.

ASSIGN SPECIFIC TIMES TO CHECK EMAILS

Don't let checking and responding to your emails hijack your day. Have designated times in your day where you will attend to your inbox, sort messages, and respond.

TRIAGE MESSAGES

When checking your messages, triage them based on priority. Handle those that require immediate response right away. For messages that require your follow-up, flag them for later action. Depending on your school's email system, you can do this in a number of ways. You might star or flag messages that you need to respond to, add a label, or move messages into an "action pending" folder.

LINK TO CALENDAR EVENTS

You can designate time to respond to a message that requires some time/follow-up by creating a calendar event specifically for it.

USE LABELS OR FOLDERS TO GROUP EMAILS

Consider grouping important messages with the same theme or source. You can do this by using labels or moving them to specific folders. You may be able to create an automatic filter that does this for you. This makes it easier to locate them later, so you can spend less time haplessly searching your inbox for that one email you need but can't seem to find.

DO AN INBOX SWEEP DAILY AND WEEKLY

Do a quick email review at the end of each day to make sure you didn't miss anything important. You can also do this once a week and make sure you have caught up with all messages and responses that you can.

SNEAK IN MAINTENANCE WHEN BORED

In line at the grocery store? On a boring commute (not driving)? Delete unnecessary messages, unsubscribe from junk mail lists, move messages to folders—and maintain some order to your inbox.

EMAIL ETIQUETTE

Emails are a professional representation of you and the main way you will correspond with the faculty members and staff at your medical school. Follow general rules for professional communication as well as some rules specific to medical students.

1. SALUTATION

Always include a salutation. Address people by their highest degree or title (Mr., Ms., Dr., Dean). Launching into an email to a faculty member or dean without a salutation is viewed as too informal and unprofessional. Take your cues from their response to determine how formal your tone should be as you continue the email conversation. When in doubt, err on the side of formality. If you are unsure whether the person you are writing to has a doctorate degree, the internet is your friend.

2. SUBJECT LINE

Make your subject line informative and clear. Do not mark "URGENT" in the subject line unless your email is truly urgent (in the case of imminent danger or serious negative effects). Ask yourself: Would the person I am writing to also consider this a drop-everything urgent request? If your message is time-sensitive, state this in the subject line, but have realistic expectations about how quickly someone will be able to respond.

3. BODY

Be concise, focused, respectful, and professional—always. Assume that any email you send could be forwarded to others.

Pro tips

WHEN SHOULD I FOLLOW UP?

You sent an email to a faculty member with a question and had hoped for a response by now. When is it appropriate to send a nudge? (This is a general guide; use your judgment.)

+ Non-urgent matter:
  3–4 weeks

+ Semi-urgent:
  1–2 weeks

+ Urgent:
  2–3 days

+ Immediate/emergent:
  1 day or call immediately

4. CLOSING

It's professional to include some kind of respectful closing, such as "Thank you," "Sincerely," or "Best."

5. SIGNATURE

Have an email signature that includes your full name, any degrees you have, and your medical school class year. You can also include your cell phone number, if you are comfortable with that, so people can contact you directly if necessary.

IMPOSTOR SYNDROME

Who does not have impostor syndrome? If you don't, consider yourself lucky; you can skip this section. If you do, welcome to the club! This psychological phenomenon is commonly seen in high-achieving people and perfectionists, which makes medical school a hotbed of impostor syndrome activity. Rampant, unfettered impostor syndrome can result in burnout and mental health issues. But you don't have to let it sabotage you and your thoughts.

Checklist for determining whether you have impostor syndrome

Do you ever think the following?

 The Admissions Committee must have made a mistake.

☑ It's only a matter of time before I'm uncovered as a complete fraud.

☑ I'm afraid of giving the wrong answer in class/small groups because people will realize that I don't know anything at all.

☑ I did OK on the exam but I got lucky this time.

 I don't deserve to be here.

PERCEPTION VERSUS REALITY

With impostor syndrome, we perceive that we know less than our colleagues and discount our abilities. In reality, everyone has their own strength areas and knowledge gaps.

What I think I know

WHAT IS IMPOSTOR SYNDROME AND DO I HAVE IT?

Impostor syndrome *(noun)*
The persistent inability to believe that one's success
is deserved or has been legitimately achieved as a result
of one's own efforts or skills.
(Oxford English Dictionary)

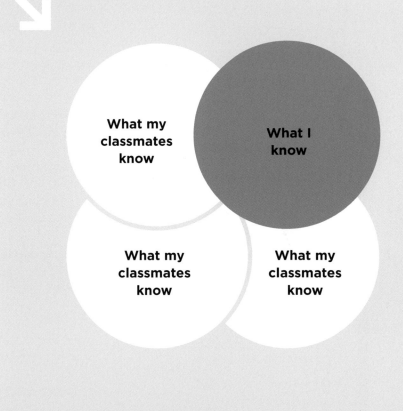

PERCEPTION | REALITY

What I think
my classmates
know

What my
classmates
know

What I
know

What my
classmates
know

What my
classmates
know

MANAGING IMPOSTOR SYNDROME

Experiencing impostor feelings is particularly common with role transitions such as starting medical school or starting the clinical phase. Yet, it can hold students back and serve as a barrier to professional growth. It may not be possible for some to fully overcome impostor syndrome, but there are ways to make it more manageable and even possibly serve as a springboard for learning. The following tips were adapted from Dr. Valerie Young, an expert on impostor syndrome.

Things a non-impostor would think

+ I am qualified for that position and will apply for it.

+ This constructive criticism will be so helpful for me to improve.

+ I did well on that exam because I studied hard and effectively.

+ I had a bad day—everyone has bad days sometimes.

+ I handled that standardized patient interaction well.

+ What can I learn today?

1. CALL IT OUT

Awareness that you are experiencing impostor syndrome is the first step. Call it what it is and know that it is a normal feeling.

2. TALK ABOUT IT

Remember that you are not alone in having these feelings. Talk about it with others—confidants, your friend group, a mentor—and normalize it.

3. SEPARATE THOUGHTS AND FEELINGS FROM TRUTH

Recognize that thoughts and feelings are not truth. Feeling like a failure does not make you a failure.

4. REFRAME FAILURE AND MISTAKES

Everyone makes mistakes. Think of every failure and mistake as a learning opportunity. Ask, "What can I learn from this?" Then, move on. Practice self-compassion.

5. BE A NON-IMPOSTOR

Fake it until you make it. When you start doubting yourself, imagine what a person without impostor feelings would think or do (see the box at left for some ideas) and think and do those things even if you are not feeling them.

6. OWN AND CELEBRATE WINS

When you do achieve a win, own and celebrate it completely. Don't qualify it or make excuses. You did it and you belong here.

"Change the dynamic of your day. Instead of dwelling on how many things you still don't know, consider how many things you could learn today."

KEY QUALITIES FOR SUCCESS

Student affairs deans assist students in their professional development throughout medical school. Here are some key qualities that student affairs deans have found lead to students succeeding in medical school. These are qualities you can cultivate over time and are not exhaustive. Note that the definition of success is individual: It is not all about graduating at the top of the class; it's about achieving personal goals and thriving in the process.

ADAPTABILITY

Adaptable students can recognize when they need to change routines or strategies in different contexts and environments. Courses may require different strategies based on content. In the clerkship years, students will need to adapt quickly to different environments.

RESILIENCE

Setbacks can and will happen. Students who use setbacks and failures as opportunities to learn and grow stronger can truly thrive during medical school. Resilience can be developed. See also Chapter Ten: Cultivating Resilience.

COLLABORATION

As a pre-med in college, there's often an über-competitive feel to things. In medical school, those who are able to work collaboratively and see peers as a source of learning and support, not competition, get more out of the process socially, emotionally, and educationally.

ORGANIZATION

Being organized and time-efficient is a must for meeting deadlines, planning study schedules, and keeping track of enriching opportunities.

CURIOSITY

Students who stay curious are always open to learning about different subjects and other people. They seek differing perspectives and possess cultural humility.

BALANCE

Staying balanced, and pursuing activities that contribute to wellness and meaning, allows students to maintain their sense of self, keep a healthy perspective, and thrive despite rigorous academic demands.

"The most successful medical students are those who are open to trying new study strategies, who actively engage with their faculty, classmates, and curriculum (rather than studying in isolation), and who recognize the value of asking for help or accessing supportive resources. Essentially, they are adaptable, flexible, willing to make mistakes and learn from them (versus expecting perfection), and resilient."

Marcy Verduin, MD, Associate Dean for Student Affairs, University of Central Florida

FIXED VERSUS GROWTH MINDSET

Carol Dweck, PhD, described two kinds of mindset: fixed and growth. People with a fixed mindset believe that qualities such as intelligence, moral character, and athletic ability are things you are born with and can't change. This is a toxic mindset for medical school! Those with a growth mindset believe that these qualities can grow and change with time, effort, and support. Thus, if they do poorly on an exam, it is not because they are not cut out for medical school (fixed mindset); it's that they need to work on improving, getting help, and finding more effective study strategies. Everyone is a mixture of both of these mindsets, but you can choose to favor growth to reach your full potential.

Fixed

+ "I need to look smart."

+ "If I have to work hard to master this material, I do not have talent or ability."

+ "I failed; I should give up."

+ "That constructive criticism got it wrong."

+ "I feel threatened by the classmates who performed better than me."

Growth

+ "I need to learn and improve."

+ "The only way to master the material is to work hard."

+ "I failed; I need to regroup and rethink my strategies."

+ "That constructive criticism will help me improve."

+ "I feel inspired by the classmates who performed better than me and hope to learn from them."

MYTHS, LEGENDS, AND PITFALLS

Here is the flip side to those qualities that help students thrive: the pitfalls. As a newbie medical student, there are certain traps to avoid in order to be as successful as possible and enjoy a productive medical school experience. If you catch yourself or your medical school friends falling into one of these often self-defeating behavior patterns, call it out.

COMPARING YOURSELF TO OTHERS

It is easily done, but comparing yourself to others simply amplifies impostor syndrome. You were admitted to medical school because you have the knowledge, skills, and attitudes necessary to become a physician. Focus on becoming the best physician possible and minimize unproductive comparisons.

NOT ASKING FOR HELP

If you find yourself flailing, ask for help. There are many support systems in place and people who want to help you succeed. Embrace a growth mindset and use all resources available to you to help you succeed. Asking for help when you need it is an act of strength, not an admission of weakness.

OVEREXTENDING

There's sometimes pressure to get involved in a ton of student organizations, interest groups, volunteer activities, research, and events, leaving you without enough time to devote to your studies. While some involvement can keep you motivated and help you round out your medical school experience, be careful not to spread yourself too thin.

PREMATURELY STRESSING OVER YOUR SPECIALTY

You do not need to know what specialty you want to pursue during the first years of medical school. If others know for sure, great for them. They may very likely change their minds. Take your time. Learn about many specialties. You do not need to make an immediate decision, or to tailor your life around a specialty too soon. You will eventually find one that fits.

"Ask yourself, 'Why am I doing this?' The goal should always be to become the best educated, most compassionate doctor you can. Keep the goal in mind and everything else will fall into place. And you'll be less distracted by the small stuff."

Kimberly Tartaglia, MD, Associate Professor of Clinical Medicine and Pediatrics, Ohio State University

Ways to stay grounded

+ Volunteer in a low-income clinic or elsewhere

+ Keep in regular touch with family and friends

+ Schedule regular social activities with friends who are not in medical school

+ Talk to a mentor or advisor

+ Engage in community service

+ Shadow a physician

+ Maintain your hobbies and interests

+ Reflect on how you got to where you are

+ Practice gratitude—write, reflect, or say what you are grateful for at the end of each day

+ Engage in the arts

+ Maintain balance

+ Embrace a sense of humor

LOSING PERSPECTIVE

When the novelty of starting medical school has started to lose its sheen and you find yourself ever deeper in the grind of preclinical exams, it is all too easy to lose perspective about what really matters and why you went to medical school in the first place. Don't close yourself off to the wider world, issues you are passionate about, and the big picture. You are going to be a doctor who can improve the lives of your patients—that's an amazing gift.

BELIEVING YOU MUST DO RESEARCH

See Chapter Seven: Research.

CHAPTER TWO

FINANCES AND BUDGETING

Medical school is an investment in your future, and an expensive one at that. Whether you are fully supported by loans, by yourself, by your family—or somewhere in between—you need to feel comfortable and in control of your financial situation. You want to be focusing on your schoolwork and your personal and professional development as a future physician and not spending excess energy worrying about money.

This requires gaining essential financial competencies, creating a sensible budget, developing disciplined spending, and—if taking out loans—understanding loan repayment options and implementing debt-management strategies. Good decisions made now can make a big difference in future years.

If reading this prior to medical school, make a start on organizing your finances, learning the basics, and getting a handle on your spending. How will you finance medical school? If you are in medical school, it's never too late to get on track. As with everything else, this is another area for your learning and growth. Your school's financial aid office can be an invaluable resource, as can financial literacy websites and professional organizations.

Remember that when you are a physician, no matter what your specialty, you will make a comfortable living and enjoy a salary much higher than most. This interlude of being a medical student and resident with limited income is temporary. Yet it is a perfect time to develop good habits. The topics outlined in this chapter—financial literacy, budgeting, and debt management—will be relevant to all of you. Your future financially secure self will thank you.

FIVE FINANCIAL ESSENTIALS

You may have been working for years prior to medical school or perhaps you have come straight from college; either way, there are five terms medical students should be familiar with in order to make sound financial decisions while studying at medical school and beyond.

1. INCOME

This is money earned through working, dividends, gifts, and so on. You must know that not all income ends up in your pocket. Some of it is taxed. Most students will not have income during medical school.

2. SAVING AND INVESTING

This is putting money aside in an interest-bearing account that allows your money to grow. Students need to know that "paying themselves first" and having a budgeted savings plan will help them meet future goals.

3. SPENDING

This is a value proposition—what you believe you need and want and how you use your limited resources (mainly money, but for a medical student this is also time) to achieve these things. Budgeting is a plan to meet these goals and to make sure that your values match your spending.

4. BORROWING

This is leveraging debt to grow assets. Students do this by taking out student loans to gain a degree, education, and experience that will have a return on investment. The goal is always to borrow the least amount of money necessary.

5. INSURING

This is protecting your assets, ensuring your ability to weather rough financial events and disabilities.

Pro tips

EMERGENCY FUND

Ideally, everyone should have an emergency fund of at least three months of expenses in their savings. This may be a tough goal to maintain during medical school but should still be a goal by the time of graduation.

In the case of an emergency, many schools have funds that can assist students in times of unexpected financial hardship. In such an event, talk to your financial aid or student affairs office for advice.

FINANCING MEDICAL SCHOOL

Medical school is an expensive investment in terms of both time and money. It can be daunting to think about how you might finance your education, but know that it can be, and has been, done by all of those before you, including those with significant premedical school debts.

SAVINGS AND GIFTS

If you have personal savings to tap into, or family members are financing some, or all, of your medical education, consider yourself fortunate! In general, it is advisable to use savings before borrowing money, unless you are earning a higher annual percentage rate in savings than that being charged on the loan.

LOANS

You will have many choices in financing your medical education, including federal loans and private loans. Federal student loans may offer higher interest rates with little to no credit check. These are good options for the risk averse and offer such benefits as the ability to forbear (temporarily suspend) payments and a choice of repayment plans. Private loans may have lower interest rates but may involve other fees and qualities that carry some risk. Discuss options with your financial aid office.

SERVICE COMMITMENT SCHOLARSHIPS

Some scholarships will pay for some or all of medical school in exchange for a future commitment, such as joining the armed services or providing primary care to communities in need.

OTHER SCHOLARSHIPS

Beyond admission scholarships, there are a multitude of institutional and external scholarships out there for the resourceful student. Some institutional scholarships are awarded based on need or other specific criteria. National professional organizations and local organizations, such as rotary clubs or religious institutions, could offer scholarships as well. You have to be willing to put in the time to search and apply for these opportunities, but it can definitely be worth your while.

PART-TIME EMPLOYMENT

Some students engage in part-time work during medical school. This can help finance your time there, but it's important to make sure that it does not interfere with academic performance or contribute to reduced well-being. If you do take a part-time position, carefully and regularly evaluate whether it remains manageable for you and a good decision overall.

BUDGETING

Budgeting is about creating a spending plan for using limited resources to achieve your needs and wants. If you haven't been disciplined about budgeting prior to medical school, now is a great time to start making informed decisions of where you spend your money. If you have loans, budgeting is essential to ensure you stay within the school-defined cost of attendance, which is based on the average cost of living and the fixed costs of your education. Think of budgeting as a tool to reach your end goal: graduating medical school with the least debt possible.

FIND THE RIGHT SYSTEM
There are many apps and tools out there to help you budget and it comes down to finding a system that works for you and that you'll stick to. Among the options are apps, calendar budgets, and spreadsheet budgets.

PUT EXTRA FUNDS TO GOOD USE
Funds not expended at the end of each month can be put into savings. If the funds are from loans, you can return them and lower your principal balance.

BUDGETING DOES NOT MEAN DEPRIVATION
Budgeting allows you to control your spending so you can spend your resources on things that you value and save elsewhere. It does not mean you must live solely on instant ramen. However, you should aim to live within your means (that is, as a student and not an attending physician yet).

Example of a phone app

Budgets October

	0%	100%	Spend	Budget	Over?
Total			**$579.50**	**$600**	**-$20.50**
Groceries			$306	$320	-$14
Restaurants			$32	$40	-$8
Clothing			$84	$80	$4
Transportation			$52.50	$50	$2.50
Fast food			$16	$20	-$4
Coffee shops			$28	$20	$8
Haircuts			$40	$40	-
Entertainment			$21	$30	-$9

USE CREDIT CARDS WISELY
Some people advise students to avoid using credit cards to ensure they stay on a budget. But credit cards do have some perks, such as helping you establish good credit by making on-time payments. Many also come with rewards, such as airline mileage or money back. The key is to make the full payment each month in order not to carry a balance. Be aware, though, that credit card debt is a huge burden and should be avoided at all costs.

Track your spending

To create a realistic budget, you need to know where you spend your money.

+ Use an app or log receipts of all of your spending in one month.

+ Categorize the examples—either as you go or at the end of the month.

+ Make use of the Budget Planner Template on page 200–201.

+ Reflect on your expenses:
  – What do you value?
  – What are important trade-offs for you?
  – What could you do without?

OCTOBER	
Week 40	
Living expenses	$120
School costs	$75
Extracurricular	$80
Week 41	
Living expenses	$365
School costs	$0
Extracurricular	$45
Week 42	
Living expenses	$120
School costs	$90
Extracurricular	$25
Week 43	
Living expenses	$1,170
School costs	$155
Extracurricular	$110
living expenses	
school costs	
extracurricular	

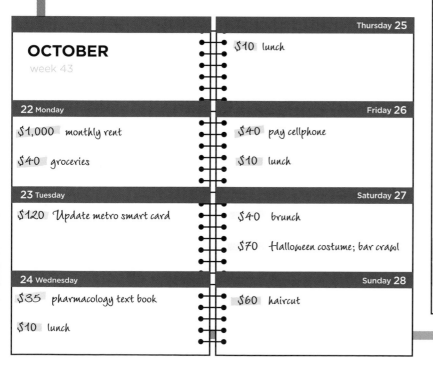

OCTOBER
week 43

22 Monday
$1,000 monthly rent
$40 groceries

23 Tuesday
$120 Update metro smart card

24 Wednesday
$35 pharmacology text book
$10 lunch

Thursday 25
$10 lunch

Friday 26
$40 pay cellphone
$10 lunch

Saturday 27
$40 brunch
$70 Halloween costume; bar crawl

Sunday 28
$60 haircut

DEBT MANAGEMENT TIPS

Think of medical school debt as an investment in your future. Remember that you are in control of your financial situation and can make good choices now that will impact you positively down the road.

DEVELOP YOUR FINANCIAL LITERACY

Empower yourself with financial literacy. Understand the effects of compound interest and the financial impacts of deferring loan repayment. Your school will likely offer debt management sessions that may be mandatory or optional. Attend these even if you don't have loans! They can teach you about critical concepts that apply to everyone. Many of you will have a mortgage someday. The same concepts apply.

BORROW ONLY WHAT YOU NEED

Don't borrow the maximum amount allowed if you won't need it, based on your budgeting and choices. A little money saved in loans now is a lot of money saved in repayment down the road. Return unused loan funds at the end of the semester.

LIVE WITHIN YOUR MEANS

Soon, you'll be living on an attending physician's salary and free to adopt a different lifestyle, but until then, live within your means as a medical student.

CONSIDER LOAN FORGIVENESS PROGRAMS

Interested in public service? You could qualify for a program that will forgive your medical student loans after a specific amount of time in public service.

APPLY FOR SCHOLARSHIPS

Every bit helps. If you don't apply for a scholarship, there's a 100% chance you won't get it.

MAKE SMART REPAYMENT DECISIONS

If you can start paying down loans, start with the loans with the highest interest rate. Some loans, such as federal loans, offer income-driven repayment plans that make payments achievable, no matter what your future resident salary. Discuss with your financial aid office and take advantage of their counseling. Explore tools such as repayment calculators to help you understand and plan for the future.

"Consider a balanced approach when repaying student loans. Income-driven repayment, if available, offers flexibility so you can consider all your financial planning needs (for example, investing/saving) during repayment. Don't assume faster is better when repaying student loans—it may not be the 'best' use of your funds if you invest wisely."

Jeffrey E. Hanson, PhD, financial literacy and borrower education consultant

"Find ways to minimize what you need to take out in the first place. Your future self will thank you for it."

PART

LEARNING AND CONTRIBUTING

CHAPTER THREE

PRECLINICAL LEARNING

The typical analogy used to describe what it is like to learn in the preclinical phase of medical school is "drinking from a fire hose." This seems like a frightening, unsustainable undertaking. Yes, there is a lot of content and it comes at you fast. Medical school often requires a new approach to learning from that used by students in college. It also demands organization, structure, time management, adaptability, and a deeper understanding of the learning process itself.

In the preclinical years, you will learn a foundation of the basic sciences upon which your future clinical practice will be built. This chapter will cover how to learn most effectively during the preclinical years, and beyond, by introducing the learning process, and ways to think about your thinking and learning (very meta), as well as providing practical, evidence-based strategies for optimizing your learning approach. This chapter will also cover lifestyle habits that aid learning, virtual learning considerations, and dedicated study periods. Running throughout the chapter, and encountered over and over, is the theme that learning is an individual process, so you should experiment to find what works for you. No two students will learn in the same way. You should expect there to be some trial and error involved. Another theme is that effective learning is hard, so you should not be afraid to do the difficult but effective things that achieve the best learning outcomes in the long run.

Medicine requires lifelong learning. Developing the optimal skills to keep learning will set you up for your career—and really anything you want to learn in the future.

THE LEARNING PROCESS

You've been learning all of these years but have you explicitly thought about the process? Many educational scholars have devoted careers to exploring the learning process and have developed various learning theories. Their insights can help you understand the basics of learning and how you can practically apply what's known to your own studies so that you can be the most effective learner possible. Let's start with the three critical components of the learning process.

A note about learning styles

There are numerous learning style inventories out there—ways to categorize how people prefer to approach learning: for example, visual, aural, kinesthetic (through physical activities). However, no studies have found that matching instruction to learning style actually improves learning. It can nevertheless be helpful to be aware of your learning preferences—your strengths and weaknesses—as you will sometimes need to engage in kinds of thinking that are less comfortable for you. Don't let that throw you.

1. COGNITIVE COMPONENT (WHAT SHOULD BE LEARNED)

This is the actual objective of the learning—the content itself, and the ways in which it needs to be structured for processing.

2. AFFECTIVE COMPONENT (WHY LEARN?)

This is your motivation to learn, your emotional relationship to the content and to your readiness to study. No motivation to learn = no learning.

3. METACOGNITIVE COMPONENT (HOW TO LEARN)

These are the skills you employ in learning: study planning, monitoring and evaluating learning progress, and identifying gaps in knowledge. Developing this component is key to optimizing your learning.

METACOGNITION

Metacognition is thinking about one's thinking. It is an awareness of how we plan, monitor, and assess our understanding and performance. Metacognitive practices allow students to assess their strengths and weaknesses as learners in different contexts, make a plan to reach learning goals, and identify and correct errors. Without metacognitive awareness, students can become overconfident and unable to identify their own weaknesses. They may not realize that their learning has been ineffective until they do poorly on an exam.

Metacognition *(noun)*
Awareness and understanding of one's own thought processes.
(Oxford English Dictionary)

Metacognitive practices

Planning

+ Before a lecture, prepare by reviewing educational objectives ahead of time.

+ Before reading, scan headings, graphs, and charts to get the big picture first.

+ Consider what you already know about the topic and what you don't know.

+ Plan out your daily study schedule.

Monitoring

+ Periodically assess learning through quizzing or recall.

+ Pre-exam: Reflect on which areas you feel most prepared and which areas you feel least prepared. Target your study accordingly.

+ Think aloud through concepts and ideas to assess understanding.

+ Create visual representations of information to delineate relationships and processes.

Assessing

+ Post-exam: Reflect on performance and plan changes to study strategies.

+ Attend exam reviews and reflect on any errors you might have made.

LEARNING AND REFLECTION

Reflection is a key part of the learning process and critical for your professional development as a physician. Reflective practice can help you develop self-awareness, emotional intelligence, empathy, critical thinking, and greater medical and interpersonal effectiveness.

You can expect many medical school assignments that aim to formally develop your capacity to reflect. This can come in the form of reflective writing assignments, learning portfolios, small-group discussions, critical incident reports, even digital media and storytelling. Regardless of the modality, the important thing is to be open to the idea—even if it doesn't feel entirely natural or within your comfort zone.

KOLB'S LEARNING CYCLE

Kolb's learning cycle involves four key stages of learning through which students move, starting with having a concrete experience, then reflecting on the experience, learning from the experience, and ending with experimentation using newfound knowledge.

Concrete Experience
(doing/having an experience)

Reflective Observation
(reviewing/reflecting on the experience)

Abstract Conceptualization
(concluding/learning from the experience)

Active Experimentation
(planning/trying out what you have learned)

RECORDING YOUR REFLECTIONS

Reflective writing is a specific type of writing. Engaging in this kind of writing may not feel particularly easy (See Step 3 below), but it does get easier with time and practice. You will likely have specific prompts or topics to address. Here are some general steps to follow when completing a reflective writing assignment. Note: Reflections are typically written in the first person and past tense.

1. DESCRIBE WHAT HAPPENED

Clearly and fully describe the incident in question. Make sure you convey all of the important details for your readers so that they feel like they are witnessing the event as it happens.

Pro tips

PUBLISHING YOUR REFLECTIONS

Some students turn their reflective writing into published essays. Medical journals, humanities journals, and various websites and blogs may have sections for reflective writing. If you think you have identified a potential scholarship opportunity, seek out a faculty member with writing experience for guidance.

2. ATTEND TO THE AFFECTIVE

How did you feel during the incident? What were you thinking? Explore the emotions you experienced.

3. ANALYZE, EXPLORE, AND CRITIQUE

Make sense of what happened. You can do this by linking the experience to past, present, and future experiences; considering the incident from multiple perspectives; identifying and challenging your assumptions, values, and biases; evaluating the experience; and imagining alternative courses of action and their potential impact.

4. IDENTIFY NEXT STEPS

Based on all of the above, what will you do the same or differently next time? How will you carry forth your insights and learning?

ACTIVE LEARNING

When we engage in active learning—as opposed to passive learning, such as simply rereading notes or re-watching a video of a lecture—we are actively constructing knowledge and understanding, which leads to more effective learning. This involves higher-order thinking. Your school's curriculum likely incorporates active learning to help you learn better. You can also maximize active learning in your approach to studying.

Examples of active learning instructional methods

+ Case-based learning

+ Team-based learning

+ Think–pair–share

+ Audience response activities

+ Discussions

+ Simulations and labs

Examples of active learning studying methods

+ Paraphrase when taking notes in a lecture

+ Teach a concept to a peer (virtual, imaginary, or in person)

+ Create concept maps (see opposite) or other visual representations of information

+ Quiz yourself and/or peers

+ Use flashcards

"Medical school in the 21st century: way too much information, not enough time. You can be overwhelmed by the number of resources out there. Success comes through finding a learning approach that works for you."

Christopher Weston, second-year medical student

CONCEPT MAPS

Concept maps are one way to organize information visually and serve as an active learning method.

Pro tips

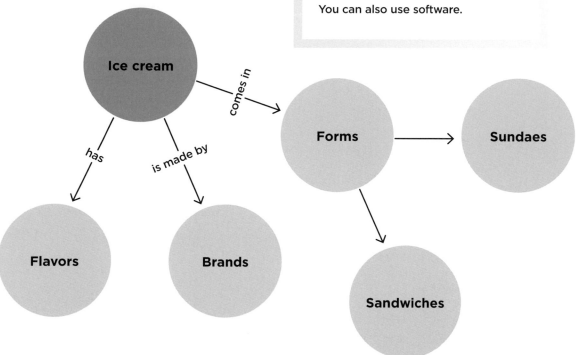

DRAWING YOUR MAP

It's OK if you have to redraw it a few times to get it right. Doing this by hand can help with long-term retention. You can also use software.

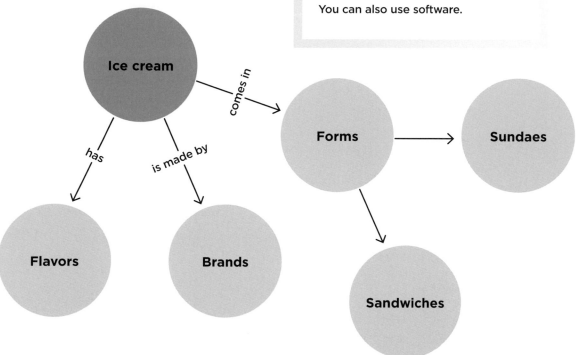

STEPS TO CONSTRUCT A CONCEPT MAP

1. List major concepts from notes or text

2. Identify the most general concepts in the list (groupings)

3. Arrange these with the most general concepts at the top:
+ Label connecting lines
+ Arrowheads can show direction, cause, and effect

4. Identify and draw cross-links between related concepts (key for integration)

5. Narrate the map aloud when done

EVIDENCE-BASED LEARNING STRATEGIES

Evidence-based learning strategies have been shown to improve long-term retention of factual knowledge. Here are three strategies to try in relation to retrieval—the process of accessing information from long-term memory.

 STRATEGY

STUDY NOTES

1. TESTING

Testing, in itself, helps students learn and is more effective than repeated studying in terms of long-term retention. Learning is maximized when testing is accompanied by feedback on why students might have gotten answers right or wrong. However, even in the absence of feedback, learning occurs to a greater degree than when simply restudying material.

+ Use question banks on content covered. If answers are available, review questions answered incorrectly or ones you were unsure about.
+ Create your own quizzes to test yourself or your peers.

2. ACTIVE RECALL

Trying to recall information instead of passively reviewing it leads to more efficient and effective learning. This is true even if the recall attempt is not successful—it stimulates subsequent learning.

+ When reviewing a lecture, try to name or write down the main facts covered even if you can't remember them entirely. Or draw/sketch the main ideas. Then revisit the material.
+ Find ways to incorporate active recall into exam study.

3. SPACED REPETITION

Retrieving content at spaced intervals (specifically, at expanding intervals from the time when it was initially learned) leads to improved long-term retention. This helps to encode facts into your long-term memory before you forget them (see opposite).

+ Design a study schedule where key content from older lectures is intentionally interspersed with newer content at expanding intervals.
+ Use apps that are specifically designed to facilitate spaced repetition.

SPACED REPETITION

The idea behind spaced repetition is that everything we memorize is on a natural "forgetting curve." By retrieving that information at increasing intervals, we alter the curve and eventually encode the material to our long-term memory.

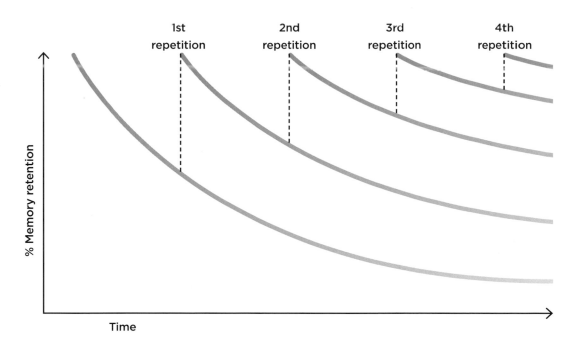

USING FLASHCARDS

Illustrated below is a method for applying spaced repetition to flashcards. Correctly answered cards are moved to the next box with an expanding frequency of your choosing. Incorrectly answered cards get moved to the first box. Apps can organize this for you electronically.

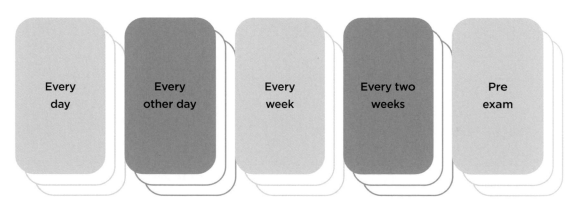

MORE EVIDENCED-BASED LEARNING STRATEGIES

Here are additional evidence-based learning strategies that have been found to enhance learning and that may also help you make important connections that deepen your understanding. Consider incorporating some of these elements into your study sessions. Note that these strategies do take more time and effort than more passive study activities—that is why they work. Think of the extra efforts involved as investments in your learning that have higher payoffs in the long run.

STRATEGY	STUDY NOTES
4. INTERLEAVING Intermixing content and types of problems, instead of studying one category at a time, produces longer-lasting learning. This may feel more difficult and learning may be more gradual in the beginning but ultimately results in better long-term outcomes.	**+** Mix content, especially content that is contrasting, in one study session. **+** Take practice exams/tests that include a variety of content, not just one topic.
5. DUAL CODING Combining verbal and visual representations of knowledge can help you remember the information better. Visual representations could be drawings, timelines, graphic organizers (see Concept Maps, page 47), or similar.	**+** From your lecture notes or assigned readings, visually represent the information. **+** Compare visuals from class material and the written materials. Write your own explanations for the visuals.
6. ELABORATIVE INTERROGATION Elaborative interrogation involves asking yourself questions about how and why things work and then finding the answers to these questions. This helps you to integrate new information and ensure deeper understanding.	**+** From a list of new content, ask questions about how and why it is connected to other ideas. **+** Explain concepts to a peer and invite their questions.

Many easy activities give you the illusion of learning. But meaningful learning is hard. It requires effort. Such 'desirable difficulty' may not feel as good, but over time it results in better learning and optimum performance.

STUDY BETTER, NOT LONGER

Many medical students struggle with their workload and find themselves sacrificing breaks and self-care activities to compensate. However, this can result in poor-quality study sessions and burnout. Building in sufficient breaks is essential for optimal focus and performance. Max Mandelbaum, postgraduate year 1 (PGY-1) in plastic surgery, offers advice on striking the right balance.

❶ Quality over quantity

I started to perform at my highest level when I began balancing my studying with healthy activities outside of work. Whether it was going to the gym, cooking evening meals, taking weekend hikes, or spending time with friends, the time away from studying helped me relax and strategically evaluate how to use my time.

❷ Consider studying with others

I found studying with a friend to be helpful in keeping me "accountable." We never quizzed each other or routinely reviewed material aloud, but it made me feel less isolated and lonesome, provided me with an available sounding board for questions/concerns regarding study material, and encouraged me to remain on task during my allotted study time.

❸ Make study time intentional

Importantly, balance did not necessarily make my studying "easier." If anything, the goal of achieving balance required me to work even harder, as I had to think critically about how I would approach my now purposefully limited study time. By approaching each study session with a plan that had to be achieved in a fixed time frame, I learned to direct my efforts in a more efficient and targeted way. Moreover, I had satisfying benchmarks each day that required me to step away from books and gave me time to digest material outside of the library.

1. Set a goal:
Decide what you want to accomplish for the session.
(1–2 minutes)

2. Study with focus and interaction:
Organize, summarize, draw concept maps, develop questions.
(30–50 minutes)

EFFECTIVE POST-CLASS STUDY SESSIONS

Here's one way to structure your study sessions from the LSU Center for Academic Success. Other schema exist; you can modify these and see what works best for you while following the general principles. Aim for three to five intense study sessions a day during the preclinical years.

3. Reward yourself with a break.
(10–15 minutes)

4. Review: Go over what you just studied.
(5 minutes)

VIRTUAL LEARNING

Virtual learning has many advantages in terms of flexibility and the delivery of expert content to broad audiences. It is sometimes a necessity. To make the most of your virtual learning experiences, it is important to be thoughtful about your learning environment and your engagement. It is all too easy to multitask or not be fully engaged during live synchronous sessions, which can lead to diminished motivation for asynchronous components. Below are some tips to help you maximize your engagement during virtual synchronous sessions, for a better learning experience overall.

1. OPTIMIZE YOUR LEARNING ENVIRONMENT

Find a quiet, calm space where you can tune out distractions and you will not be interrupted. Turn off notifications on your phone or computer. Ensure there is stable, strong internet/Wi-Fi access.

2. BE PREPARED AND PUNCTUAL

Sign in early to virtual learning sessions, especially prior to the first session, to make sure your microphone and/or camera is working and you do not have any issues accessing the platform.

3. BE SEEN

If turning on your video camera is an option, and encouraged, use it when possible. It's easier to be distracted and multitask when you are off-camera. It also helps your instructor know you are engaged and tracking everything.

4. ASK QUESTIONS

Use the chat function, raise your virtual hand, or send a private message to the presenter whenever anything is unclear. This not only helps you pay attention and stay engaged with the content, it also communicates to your instructor that you are there to learn. Be sure to use appropriate and professional communication, just as you would in a physical class.

5. PARTICIPATE

If there are interactive elements to the session, such as separate breakout room discussions or participatory activities such as writing on a virtual whiteboard, participate fully. This helps you work better with concepts, your co-learners, and instructors, and thus helps your learning.

6. CONTINUE THE CONVERSATION

After the session, keep the conversation going with your peers and even your instructor. You can share resources or collaborate further. This can extend the learning experience and add value for you and for your classmates.

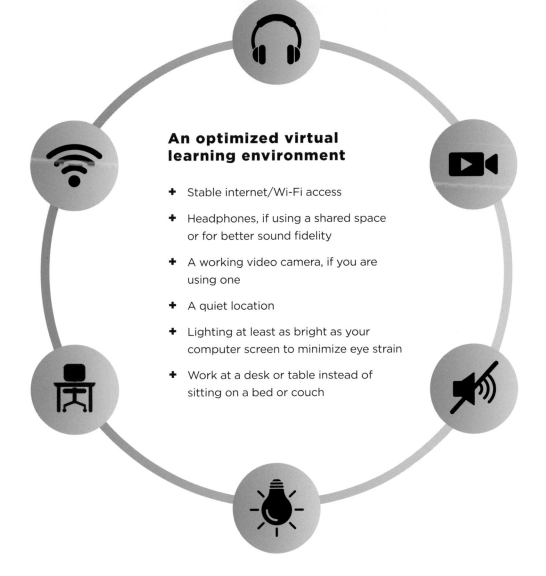

An optimized virtual learning environment

+ Stable internet/Wi-Fi access

+ Headphones, if using a shared space or for better sound fidelity

+ A working video camera, if you are using one

+ A quiet location

+ Lighting at least as bright as your computer screen to minimize eye strain

+ Work at a desk or table instead of sitting on a bed or couch

"Give a virtual course the same interest, focus, and work ethic as you would a course where you are interacting with your preceptors in person. I would suggest asking questions, chiming in on discussions, and actively following along during presentations. This makes the experience worthwhile, because when you are just passively listening, it's very easy to zone out."

Brittney Gordon, fourth-year medical student

LIFESTYLE HABITS THAT AID LEARNING

While creating a study plan and schedule to make the most of evidence-based learning strategies and active learning, make sure to factor in lifestyle habits that are known to promote learning. Many medical students focus on the former without paying attention to the latter, and this is akin to leaving learning "money" on the table.

 SLEEP

Need another excuse to sleep? Sleep helps you consolidate memories. There's also evidence that sleep not only helps you remember information but also improves your ability to understand and apply that information. Feel no guilt about sleeping. Prioritize good sleep for your learning and general health.

 EXERCISE

Regular aerobic exercise helps you learn in multiple ways. It helps to improve your alertness, attention, and readiness to learn. In addition, from a neuroscience perspective, it facilitates neural connections and the development of new neurons in the hippocampus— essential for memory. Not to mention its other advantages of improving sleep, as well as decreasing stress and anxiety (among so many other benefits). All of this results in improved thinking and learning.

Sleep dos and don'ts

+ Use your bed for sleeping only (not studying or working).

+ Avoid caffeine in the evening.

+ Avoid large meals and alcohol before bed.

+ Set a regular sleep schedule.

+ Aim for 7.5–9 hours of sleep a night.

+ Avoid blue light (from smartphones and computers) for 2 hours before bed.

+ Exercise during the day.

+ Limit naps to 30 minutes.

+ Ensure exposure to natural light during the day (that means no marathon basement library study sessions).

EAT WELL

It makes sense that ensuring a healthy, regular diet can nourish both body and mind. It's hard to focus when you are hungry. Students who eat breakfast regularly seem to have better academic success, according to studies. In addition, a diet high in trans and saturated fats may result in poorer performance overall.

TAKE A MIND BREAK

Try studying for hours on end and you'll recognize how inefficient and unpleasant it becomes. True breaks allow our brains to go from a focused mode of thinking to a diffuse mode. Diffuse mode is like the app on your phone that is running in the background: It's still processing and making connections without you knowing. This is why you have such great ideas and come up with solutions to problems when you wake up in the morning or while taking a shower. We need to alternate between both modes of thinking to make important cognitive connections and solve problems. See the box for some mind break activities you could try.

When to take a mind break:

+ In between study sessions: Take a 10–15-minute break where your mind can wander.
+ Taking an exam and can't answer a question?: Move to the next question after 1–2 minutes and return to it later.
+ During a study session when you are struggling with a concept: Switch to different content and return during a later session.

Mind breaks for diffuse thinking

+ Nap/sleep
+ Exercise/play a sport
+ Go for a walk
+ Play a game on your phone
+ Daydream
+ Go for a drive
+ Meditate
+ Listen to music (especially without lyrics)

OPTIMIZE WELL-BEING

You can't learn optimally if you are not taking care of yourself in terms of your physical, mental, social, financial, and emotional well-being. Untreated mental health or physical issues, financial distress, or an unsafe living situation can impair your ability to learn. Invest in activities that improve your well-being in all dimensions in order to be the most effective medical student you can be. See also Chapter Nine: Optimizing Well-Being for Medical School Success.

DEDICATED STUDY PERIODS

Dedicated study periods for board exams require thoughtful planning. Think of them as customizable blocks of time that should be tailored to you. Try not to be overly concerned with how others are studying—there are many pathways to success. Keep in mind that these periods can be a great time to synthesize and consolidate your learning, which will only help you be a better doctor in the future. Here are some tips for planning dedicated study periods.

REFLECT AND SELF-ASSESS

What are the most effective study strategies for you? What are your preferences for learning and structuring your day? Which content areas are your strengths and which are weak points that will require extra attention?

PLAN OUT GENERAL TIME REQUIREMENTS

For how many weeks will you study? You want to have sufficient time but not too long (this can lead to burnout and lower performance). How many days per week will you study? How many hours per day? Give yourself at least one day completely free. Factor in the need for breaks and the lifestyle habits that you need to be healthy and at your most productive. Build in flex time for unexpected setbacks and/or extra self-care needs that arise.

DECIDE ON RESOURCES

At a minimum, you will need something for content review, test questions, and practice tests. Find out what your more senior peers used and why, while being aware that this is an individual decision.

PLAN OUT YOUR WEEKLY AND DAILY SCHEDULES

At what times of day are you at your most focused? Which evidence-based strategies will you use to maximize your learning each day? For instance, will you interleave content areas within a single study session? Will you plan to study harder topics earlier in the day? Will you incorporate spaced repetition? How many practice questions will you do? Use practice questions to identify weak areas early on to target your study.

INCORPORATE TESTING

Practice exams can help you assess your learning progress and simulate exam conditions. Please be aware that progress may not be linear. It's too easy to get discouraged by lack of hoped-for progress on practice exams, which may not reflect your true progress or actual final score. Use more than a single practice exam score as a measure of your learning. Embrace a growth mindset and trust the process.

OTHER

Where will you study? Will you incorporate study with others? Who will be your supports during the day? How will you integrate needed outside interactions with friends, family, and the world?

APPROACH TO BOARDS

For some students, dedicated study periods can be stressful, isolating, and the cause of burnout. They don't have to be. Some students are able to find balance and stay grounded during this time while engaging in productive and effective learning. Fourth-year medical student Rose Milando explains how she made it work for her.

❶ Learn how you learn

Give yourself enough time, do the pre-work of understanding how you learn, and build a schedule that allows you to cover the material in a way that works for you, with NBME practice tests along the way to evaluate your progress.

❷ Know when to stop

For me, come 6 or 7pm, I couldn't retain any more information, no matter how hard I tried. And instead of making myself feel bad about that, or pushing myself to study even if I was not learning, I accepted it as a fact and planned my schedule around it. I would make dinner with my cousin, or take the dog for a walk, or watch TV for the rest of the evening. That way, I never felt truly burned out, or guilty for "failing," or guilty for "indulging" in socializing with friends or family.

❸ Stay connected with what gives you meaning

It was important for me to view studying as something I was deeply committed to, but not something that cost me everything else. I made a point to keep working on projects that were meaningful and important to me, even if at a reduced capacity. My classmates and mentors knew I was studying, so I set low, manageable expectations, and met via Zoom once a week or so to check in—even just to say, "I wasn't able to get to that this week. Let's try again next week." This approach to research and socializing during my dedicated study period allowed me to feel connected to the things I love and care about, which for me is the only way to avoid resentment, burnout, and ultimately poor performance.

❹ Finding what works

If the resources and/or study approach are not working for you, do not feel obligated to stick with them. Engage your metacognitive processes to assess your learning regularly. When feeling stuck, reach out to an advisor or learning specialist for guidance to get back on track.

CHAPTER FOUR

CONTRIBUTING TO TEAMS

By the time you are in medical school, you've likely been part of many teams, from sports teams to class project teams, and possibly work teams and research teams. Some teams probably worked really well together and others might have been laden with dysfunction. Be honest: Did you complete the class group assignment largely by yourself since no one else was contributing and it was just easier that way?

Teamwork in medicine is critical. On a patient care team, you will be part of a group that must work well together in order to deliver safe, high-quality patient care. You will need to work with people with different personalities, work styles, and backgrounds. Team dysfunction in this setting can be disastrous; mistakes and miscommunication can lead to poor clinical outcomes. Residency program directors are therefore looking for applicants who can contribute positively to teams and who have the interpersonal skills to overcome team conflict and challenges. You'll have the opportunity to work in teams throughout medical school to help you develop these crucial teamwork skills. For some, it means putting aside ego and embracing humility and shared, collective outcomes over individual achievement.

This chapter is about understanding how teams function most effectively and how you can positively contribute to them, both as a team member and as a leader. Regardless of your role on a team, you can help support the team to stay on track, develop social bonds, diagnose dysfunction, and manage conflict. As a team member, you can also learn to give and receive effective feedback like a pro. These teamwork and leadership skills will set you up well for residency and your practice in the years to come.

STAGES OF TEAM DEVELOPMENT

One approach to understanding teams focuses on the stages groups go through. The best known of these was developed by psychologist Bruce Tuckman and is shown below. Teams go through a set of predictable stages before they start performing. Acknowledging these stages can help you understand and contribute to the development of your teams. Note that progression may not always be linear, and teams can and do regress to earlier stages at times. Some teams also get stuck at certain stages, with a resulting impact on performance.

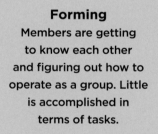

Forming
Members are getting to know each other and figuring out how to operate as a group. Little is accomplished in terms of tasks.

Storming
Conflicts arise. There may be uncertainty or disagreement about roles, project requirements, or procedures. It can feel like the team is failing.

There are some key takeaways from this team development theory that you can apply to the teams you belong to. Knowing what to expect and what is normal can lessen team-induced stress as well as help you to support your team to achieve greater success.

The first takeaway is that the getting-to-know-each-other phase is important for the team's overall performance. Time invested in the forming stage is well spent, even if things aren't getting done from a task perspective. Secondly, there is no need to panic if conflicts arise.

Pro tips

EXPEDITING TEAM DEVELOPMENT

Some teams must come together rapidly and start performing right away. Think of a ward team in a hospital with residents, interns, students, and an attending physician, all of whom must work together to start providing safe, evidence-based care right away.

By attending to team development stages, your team can more rapidly cycle through them, ensuring team members get to know one another and establish clear roles and norms from the beginning.

Norming

The team starts to organize around a group identity and clarified individual roles. Cohesiveness develops. New standards and ground rules are established.

Performing

The team is actively performing and work is moving forward toward the collective goal. The team is collaborative, efficient, and productive.

They are often a necessary part of working out kinks and clarifying roles and processes. Expect conflict and work through it together. Thirdly, it takes time to get to the performing stage. There's groundwork to lay, conflict to resolve, bonds to establish.

There is, in fact, one final stage in this team development theory—adjourning—but that should be self-explanatory.

ELEMENTS OF SUCCESSFUL TEAMS

To form a successful, well-performing team, you need to have certain elements in place. Some of these elements can be ensured by thoughtful planning as the team comes together (see opposite), while others have to do with interpersonal dynamics.

SHARED PURPOSE

Teams must share a clear and common purpose that each team member can articulate and be committed to achieving. Note, a team's purpose can change over time and it's important that everyone is on board with the change.

CLEAR ROLES AND RESPONSIBILITIES

Each team member understands their role in the team and the roles and contributions of other team members.

EFFECTIVE COMMUNICATION

Communication between team members is open, full, and accurate, with all key members included. Team members show mutual respect to one another and can express disagreement or diverse viewpoints freely without fear of being shut down.

APPROPRIATE LEADERSHIP

A team needs leadership to accomplish its goals but leadership need not reside with a single person (see Team Leadership Functions, pages 66–67).

TRUST

Trust is paramount to a team's successful functioning and collaboration. Each member is committed to the success of the team and, as a group, they can manage conflicts and problem-solve effectively. Each member understands and respects the norms of the team.

Pro tips

COGNITIVE DIVERSITY

One other component that can contribute to a team's effectiveness is cognitive diversity. Different perspectives help teams make good decisions. Diversity of thought can lead to conflict if team members do not try to understand each other's perspectives and work together to use this diversity of opinion as an opportunity, not a challenge.

TEAM CHARTER

A team charter is a written document that outlines a team's purpose, scope, objectives, and timelines. This is created by the whole team and helps establish shared goals, buy-in, and accountability. A charter can be ongoing or cover a specified period of time, for example, a year or semester. It can look however you like—the important thing is having a collaborative, agreed-upon "guiding star."

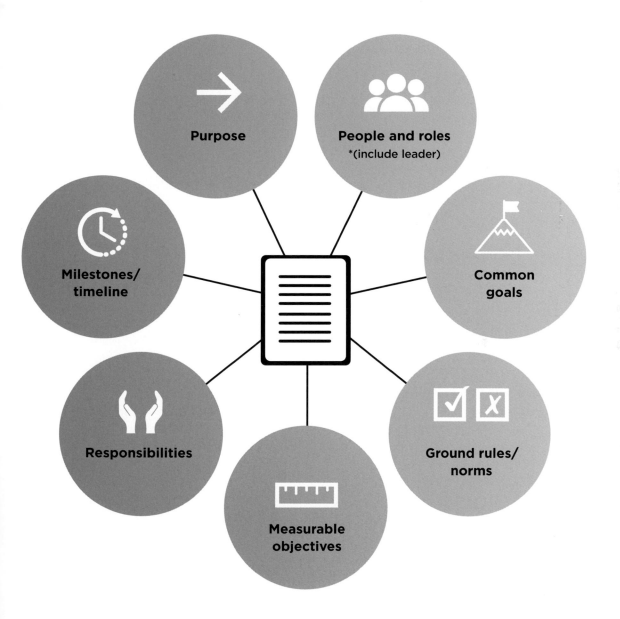

TEAM LEADERSHIP FUNCTIONS

Every team needs formal or informal leadership to be effective. There may be multiple people within a team who fulfill leadership functions to help the team meet its goals. A team leader will need to:

ESTABLISH THE TEAM

If you are building a team from scratch, you may need to select team members with the right knowledge, experience, and skills to accomplish the team's goals. Often, though, you will be working with a team that is already formed/assigned. In this case, a leader will assess the capabilities of the current members and perhaps recruit additional members if needed, or reassign roles to make the best use of people's skills and strengths.

DEFINE MISSION OR PURPOSE

You will need to define and communicate the team's mission or purpose clearly so that there is a shared understanding and commitment to the team's work. This helps a team form a common identity and cohesiveness.

ESTABLISH EXPECTATIONS AND GOALS

Help the team establish goals. The goal-setting process can be shared among team members. How will members be accountable for ensuring that the team meets its goals?

PLAN PROCESSES

What is the best way to structure the team and carry out processes to meet your goals? Figure out the division of labor, how the work will be done, and the timeline. Consider team involvement in this phase, asking members for their input to encourage buy-in.

MONITOR, PROBLEM-SOLVE, FRAME

A team leader needs to monitor a team's progress and intervene when necessary to help a team that is performing poorly or has lost sight of its goals. You may encourage team members to resolve issues themselves or you may coach a team through challenges yourself. When events occur (internal or external) that threaten the team's work, help members to understand what it may mean for the team and to cope with any fallout.

SUPPORT SOCIAL CLIMATE

Social relationships and interpersonal dynamics within a team are key to its smooth functioning and eventual success. Do team members feel safe, respected, and unified toward the team's mission? Can team members express their disagreement or voice opposing views safely? A good team leader will look out for individual members and their well-being.

Running an effective team meeting

Before the meeting

+ Plan meeting objective(s)

+ Prepare an agenda considering what needs to be accomplished and how long it will take

+ Consider sharing relevant information in advance to maximize time during the meeting

During the meeting

+ Respect everyone's time—start and end the meeting on time and don't recap at length for latecomers

+ Follow the agenda but allow for flexibility and on-the-fly adaptation if needed

+ Help the meeting stay on topic

+ Summarize next steps at the end of the meeting

After the meeting

+ Send out a summary of the meeting, including who is assigned what actions and within what time frame

+ Reflect on how the meeting went, whether the objectives were met, and what you might want to do differently next time

---

"While one of our biggest roles in medical school is as a learner, we are also quickly challenged to lead—both inside and outside of clinical settings. Taking on a leadership role can be immensely rewarding and have a positive impact on your development as a clinician."

Harleen Marwah, fourth-year medical student

DEVELOPING YOURSELF AS A LEADER

Leadership is really about influencing others and isn't tied to a role or title. Physicians are leaders and you can develop the necessary skills and competencies required to become a better leader. Critical to this process is understanding your strengths and areas you need to develop to be most effective. Use the guide below to think about what those areas might be.

Mark areas of **strength (S)** and areas you want to work on **developing (D)**

PERSONAL QUALITIES AND EMOTIONAL INTELLIGENCE

+ Self-awareness
+ Cultural sensitivity
+ Professionalism
+ Empathy
+ Continuing personal development

COMMUNICATION SKILLS

+ Listening
+ Clear articulation of ideas—spoken
+ Clear articulation of ideas—written
+ Influencing

MANAGERIAL SKILLS

+ Delegating
+ Conflict management
+ Negotiation
+ Organization
+ Time management

TEAMWORK

+ Visioning
+ Relationship-building
+ Facilitating group discussion
+ Goal-setting
+ Giving and receiving feedback

To be a good leader, we have to understand who we are as a person, what are our strengths, and where we need to commit ourselves to improvement.

CAUSES OF TEAM DYSFUNCTION

Patrick Lencioni, author and president of a management consultancy firm, describes an interrelated model of the causes of team dysfunction. Each level of dysfunction builds upon the one(s) below. For instance, if team members don't trust one another, they can't openly debate issues for fear of creating conflict. Team leaders can be aware of these causes and work to make teams more functional, cohesive, and high-performing.

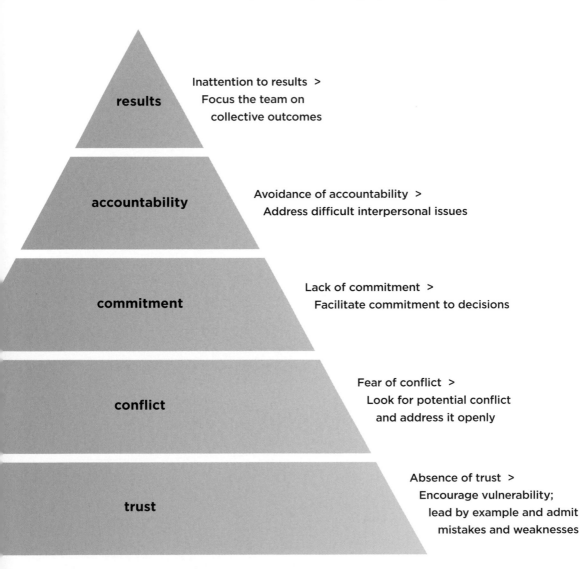

results — Inattention to results > Focus the team on collective outcomes

accountability — Avoidance of accountability > Address difficult interpersonal issues

commitment — Lack of commitment > Facilitate commitment to decisions

conflict — Fear of conflict > Look for potential conflict and address it openly

trust — Absence of trust > Encourage vulnerability; lead by example and admit mistakes and weaknesses

RESOLVING TEAM CONFLICT

Conflict is a normal part of teamwork (and life) but, if left unaddressed, can jeopardize team function and team member satisfaction. Different personalities, work styles, leadership style preferences, and task-related issues can give rise to team conflicts. Whether you are directly involved in the conflict or a team member bystander, you can help the team resolve its conflicts to get back on track.

1. STAY CALM AND CARRY ON
Conflict can make us uncomfortable or defensive at times and cause us to want to flee the scene. However, it needs to be addressed calmly and professionally, and the sooner the better.

2. ACKNOWLEDGE THE CONFLICT
Facilitate an open dialogue in a safe place. Acknowledge the conflict in nonjudgmental terms. What is happening and what is the impact on the team?

3. LISTEN AND SEEK UNDERSTANDING
The most important step is for everyone to listen to one another. Listen attentively and empathetically to all sides. Seek everyone's full understanding of all positions. What are everyone's hopes, concerns, and fears? Resist early judgments and remember to stay calm.

4. FIND A RESOLUTION
What are the things that everyone can agree on? What are the shared interests? Brainstorm solutions and see if there are any win-win situations. As a group, come up with a resolution that everyone is comfortable with.

5. INVOLVE A THIRD PARTY
If a resolution can't be found, involve a neutral third party who can mediate and help the team overcome the conflict. This could be a faculty member, peer, dean, or somebody else, depending on the situation.

GIVING FEEDBACK

Giving and receiving feedback are essential skills for team membership and leadership. The way you deliver feedback will impact the way it is received and whether or not it is taken on board. Remember: Always give feedback from a caring place.

1. PICK THE RIGHT TIME AND PLACE

Feedback is most helpful if it is given in a timely manner and in the right setting. The environment should be quiet and private when possible and, if delivering feedback in the group setting, it should be considered a safe, respectful space.

2. ASK FOR SELF-ASSESSMENT

How did the person feel about their performance? What did they feel went well and what didn't?

3. PROVIDE SPECIFIC FEEDBACK

Aim for balanced feedback based on observations. Include what has gone well, being as detailed as possible. For areas of improvement, focus on specific modifiable behaviors. Limit your feedback to one or two areas for improvement. Be nonjudgmental and respectful, focusing on behaviors and not the person. Remember how hard it is for some people to accept constructive feedback. Deliver it as you would like someone to deliver it to you.

4. CHECK BACK IN

Assess the person's understanding and reception of the feedback. Help clarify any aspects of your feedback that weren't clear.

The lowdown on the feedback sandwich

The "feedback sandwich" is one recognized way to deliver feedback. The "buns" are positive sentiments and the "meat" represents negative observations/areas for improvement. The feedback sandwich used to be all the rage but it has fallen out of favor with many, since it can end up sounding insincere and contrived when done poorly. It can also minimize the reception of negative feedback by watering it down. Some still find the general approach helpful when done well, so you could always test it out, aiming to be as genuine as possible. You could also try a low-carb variation and leave out the bottom bun.

positive

negative

positive

RECEIVING FEEDBACK

Do you receive feedback with grace and gratitude? Or do you dread receiving it? Hopefully, the person giving you feedback has approached the task with thoughtfulness and intention but, even if not, there is a way to extract value and use it to improve.

1. MENTALLY PREPARE

The moment you know you are going to be receiving feedback, pause for a second and remember that feedback will help you grow. Go into the conversation or session with an open, objective mind: Your goal is to extract helpful information about your performance without taking any of the feedback personally.

2. ACTIVELY LISTEN

Listen carefully to what is being said and allow the person to share their thoughts without interruption. Also pay attention to any emotional content being conveyed through tone, choice of words, and other nonverbal cues. Repeat back what you have heard to check whether you've understood it correctly.

3. CLARIFY

Seek to understand fully by clarifying points that are unclear and asking for specific examples if you need them. Try not to question the feedback at this point.

4. EXPRESS GRATITUDE

No matter what it is, thank the person for sharing their feedback. It's not easy to give feedback. However you feel about a person's assessment of you, acknowledge their effort.

5. PROCESS

Either during the feedback session or afterward, take time to deconstruct the comments made. How can you incorporate the feedback to improve? Were the comments different from what you have previously been told? If so, why? Before you write off feedback as invalid, consider honestly whether there are elements of truth that require you to make changes. Someone may have an incorrect perception of your behavior—but perceptions are important too. Seek to find the truth and grow as a result.

Pro tips

ACCEPTING FEEDBACK

If, at any time, you start to feel defensive and crushed, remember that it's a natural response but not productive. Take a mental step back, breathe slowly, and detach from those personal feelings as best as you can. And whatever you do, do not argue about the feedback, even if you disagree. Receive it gracefully. Fully process it later.

CHAPTER FIVE

SUMMERS AND BREAKS

You have worked hard, amassing an amazing amount of knowledge and many new skills—you deserve each and every break that comes along during medical school. How will you spend them?

Dr. Thomas Koenig, a wise student affairs dean, once said, "Medicine tries to obey Boyle's Law. It will expand to fill all available space if you let it"—see page 85 for more from Dr. Koenig. Summers and breaks are a great time to practice setting boundaries on how much space you want medicine to fill and how.

Many medical schools have just one summer break, and there is a lot of pressure for students to "make it count" and be academically productive. This can be a good time to engage in research or other professional pursuits. However, it's important not to forget that you need a break too, and to devote time to things that you need to do for your own well-being, to recover, and to be prepared for the times ahead in school.

This chapter considers ways in which to plan summers and breaks and looks at some of the activities that students may choose to participate in. Keep in mind that there are no right answers and you should individualize your plans based on your personal situation and goals, and what you want and need.

PLANNING YOUR SUMMER

Planning your summer can be daunting, but as with all things in medical school, reflection and forethought go a long way to help you prepare. Remember that plans can and do change—keep your aims in mind and be adaptable. There are many ways to reach your goals.

WHEN TO START

It's not too early to start thinking about summer plans in November or December of first year, even though it will seem as though you only just started medical school. The reason is that some summer internships and research positions or scholarships will have deadlines in January or even December. Take some time to consider your options.

CONSIDER YOUR GOALS

Reflect on your goals. Are you set on becoming a plastic surgeon or another über-competitive specialty that is research-heavy? In that case, you might want to do research (See Chapter Seven: Research). Is one of your goals to be home during the summer, for family or financial reasons? Is one of your goals to engage in career exploration? Travel? Wellness? All of the above?

DETERMINE YOUR REQUIREMENTS

Do you have any activities that need to be accomplished over the summer? Military scholarship students may need to do officer training, for example. Those in research or scholarly concentration programs may need to complete projects or internships.

EXPLORE POSSIBILITIES

Explore the universe of possibilities based on your goals and requirements. Your school will likely have resources to help with this. Talk to older peers and advisors. It's OK if this process takes you a little while—some summer plans come together quickly and others take months to develop. Either way, with some thought and guidance, you can make the most of the time.

APPLY FOR INTERNSHIPS AND FUNDING

If you intend to apply for any opportunities that require applications, such as internships or scholarships, do so by the deadlines.

"During your semesters of medical school you learned how to prepare and study. During the summer you will learn how to self-reflect and recover. All four elements are necessary for walking the path of a physician, so don't short-cut the process."

Lorenzo Norris, MD, Associate Dean for Student Affairs, George Washington University

Summer priorities

What are your priorities for the summer? You can think about them in terms of four categories. What are your highest priorities and needs?

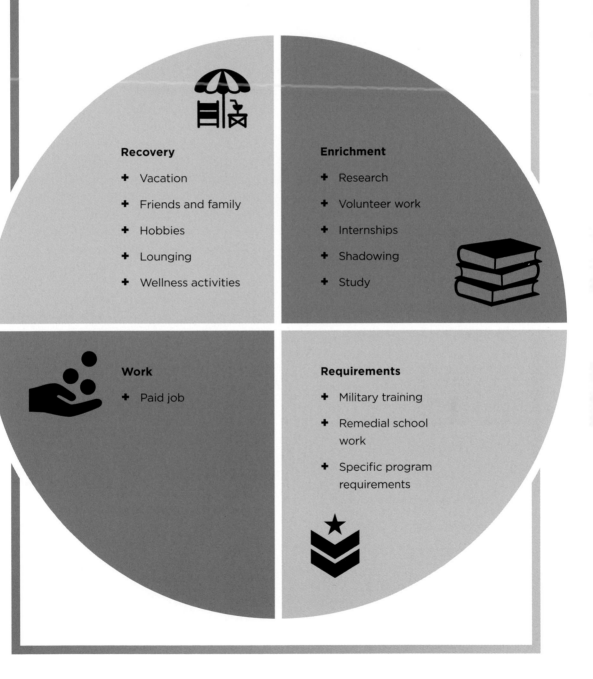

Recovery

+ Vacation
+ Friends and family
+ Hobbies
+ Lounging
+ Wellness activities

Enrichment

+ Research
+ Volunteer work
+ Internships
+ Shadowing
+ Study

Work

+ Paid job

Requirements

+ Military training
+ Remedial school work
+ Specific program requirements

INTERNATIONAL EXPERIENCES

Summers and breaks offer potential time to travel internationally, for either service, clinical, research, and/or immersive language experiences. Some schools plan international service trips around spring breaks. These experiences can provide valuable perspectives on global health and providing care in lower-resourced countries but do need to be thoughtfully planned.

CHOOSE VETTED PROGRAMS

Go through your medical school's international office to select opportunities that have been pre-screened and vetted for educational benefit and safety. This includes pre-departure and post-departure counseling. Students can find themselves in ethically difficult situations overseas, including being placed in clinical settings with inadequate oversight; long-standing programs lessen this risk.

Budgeting expenses

You'll need to make a detailed list of expenses to create a budget and to help you determine your funding needs. Some major elements include:

+ Visas, passport

+ Transportation

+ Elective travel insurance

+ Accommodation and food

+ Immunizations

+ Cell phone plans

+ Program fees

SELECT THE RIGHT PROGRAM FOR YOU

Reflect on your objectives. Do you need structure or do you prefer to be more independent? Keep in mind that in a different country, more structure can be helpful, particularly if you are doing research. Consider language and the costs involved. Your personal safety is paramount, so be sure to check any travel advisories and research the political situation in the area.

CONSIDER FUNDING OPTIONS

International travel is expensive, so you may need to seek a scholarship or loan to cover expenses. These could be offered through your school, financial institutions, religious institutions, charities, professional organizations, or even local businesses. You may also fundraise and pool a number of resources together.

BE FLEXIBLE

International electives and experiences can and do fall through, sometimes at the last minute. World events can change situations quickly. Be cautiously optimistic and stay on top of events happening at home and abroad that could impact your trip. Travel insurance and refundable tickets could be smart moves.

AN ENRICHING SUMMER

Fourth-year medical student Harleen Marwah describes how she decided what to do over the summer, faced with a number of exciting and varied opportunities. The end result was a fulfilling, enriching experience.

Step outside your comfort zone

Our medical school circulated opportunities in research, policy, entrepreneurship, advocacy, and more. Since I had worked in international policy prior to medical school, I was immediately drawn to a number of these opportunities, but I realized that many were similar to experiences I had already had. I took a step back to think critically about what I might do differently now as a medical student.

❷ Fulfill personal and professional goals

After evaluating my prior experiences and thinking about new skills I wanted to build, I decided to spend my summer in India engaging in clinical observation and research in maternal and child health. Working in India fulfilled both personal and professional goals. Professionally, I have an interest in clinical careers in global health. Personally, I had never traveled to India, even though I am a first-generation Indian-American from a Sikh family. I was eager to learn about my own heritage and explore more deeply a culture that has shaped much of my life.

Seek meaningful experiences

One of my most valuable lessons from this summer was seeing first-hand that, across the world, we all share a similar human condition. People living in a variety of circumstances search for joy, meaning, and purpose. Before going to India, I was nervous, but I left feeling humbled and empowered. I will not let this experience and opportunity go to waste. I will use it to fuel my clinical practice, inform my goals, and shape my perspective moving forward.

SHADOWING

Shadowing as a premedical student may have helped you decide whether you wanted to pursue a medical career. In medical school, it can help you learn about specific specialties and discover what you would and would not like to incorporate in your future medical career. Some students do this during the school year, but it can be challenging to balance. It may be preferable to undertake some shadowing during the summer, when your schedule is lighter. This could be done in person or even virtually in some cases.

FIND A PHYSICIAN (OR PHYSICIANS) TO SHADOW

Your school may offer a shadowing program for preclinical students for which they have already solicited faculty who would like to participate. If not, you could identify someone through referral from older students, the dean's office, faculty advisors, or your own research. You may want to find a physician in a specialty you have interest in, or simply a physician who is known to be a good mentor. Either way, you can learn a lot about clinical interactions and gain insights on specialty choice. You can shadow multiple physicians or try to develop a closer relationship with just one.

PARTICIPATE PROFESSIONALLY

Arrive early. Be prepared by reading about the specialty ahead of time. Dress professionally. Jot down questions for opportune times. Treat all patients and staff with respect. Some patients may not want students present during the visit—handle this gracefully. You can use the time instead to look up pertinent information, or note down any questions you may have.

DEBRIEF

If there's time at the end of your session, the person you are shadowing (your preceptor) will often be available to debrief and answer any queries you may have from the session. Save questions that you can easily look up at home for later. If you'll be joining this person in the future, see if you should do anything differently next time. Remember to thank your preceptor.

REFLECT

Take time to think (or write) about what you liked or did not like about what you saw. What was most interesting to you? What did you learn about clinical medicine? Patient–physician interactions? This specialty? Are there things you still want to know?

Virtual shadowing

Before the session:

+ Contact the person you'll be shadowing prior to your session to understand procedures and expectations:

  - How will you communicate during the session?

  - What should you do if you have technical difficulties?

  - Will you strictly be observing or are you expected to participate?

+ Do some reading/research about your preceptor's specialty—typical cases, patient population, and so on.

+ Choose an environment that is private with adequate lighting. Ideally, use headphones.

During the session:

+ Log in early to make sure your equipment is working.

+ Dress professionally, as you would for an in-person session.

+ Be completely engaged—do not attempt to multitask; turn off your phone/email notifications.

+ Jot down questions for later.

After the session:

+ Thank your preceptor and ask any questions.

+ If you will shadow this person again, ask whether you should do anything differently.

+ Read up on anything you saw that you would like to know more about.

+ Reflect on your thoughts about the specialty—what did you find interesting or meaningful?

STUDYING

Many students wonder if they should study during their summer break. For most, studying should not be a priority of the summer, which should mainly be about recharging, reflecting, and potentially pursuing other meaningful experiences. Some students will feel extremely uncomfortable not studying at all for board exams or otherwise. Here are some situations in which studying could be incorporated into summer plans.

FORMAL REMEDIATION

If you had an academic stumble and need to remediate a course or courses, the summer can allow you time to catch up. Approach this with a growth mindset—this is your opportunity to grow, learn, and fortify your foundation of knowledge. Stick to a structured study schedule and make sure you take the necessary breaks, incorporating the strategies and self-care that are covered in Chapter Three: Preclinical Learning.

REVIEW WEAK AREAS

As the pace of medical school is fast, there may have been specific subjects or processes that you never felt like you mastered or fully "got" the first time around. The summer could be a time to review and strengthen your understanding of these areas.

BOARDS PREP

Your boards may be a long way off, which makes earnest studying during the summer lower yield. You will have a dedicated study period for that preparation. However, some students like to start early and may choose to do practice questions or review high-yield content in pharmacology, pathology, and physiology in the organ systems already covered.

FOCUSED STUDY USING SUMMER EXPERIENCE

If engaged in a research project, shadowing, volunteering, or global health work, you could focus study on directly connecting your learning to those experiences. For instance, drawing connections, if relevant, to what you have learned so far in medical school with the topics you are engaging with during the summer organically. This can help anchor your learning and make it more intentional.

Pro tips

GIVE YOURSELF
A BREAK

Remember, for most students, studying over the summer and during breaks is not necessary.

BREAKS

Besides the summer, there are various other breaks during the medical school year. As these are shorter, it is more important to use these times for rest, recovery, reflection, and self-care versus more ambitious enrichment plans. For some, though, spending dedicated time doing something that connects you to why you wanted to be a doctor in the first place may be part of your rest and recovery process.

Holiday breaks: Students may decide to travel home to be with family or celebrate with friends at school.

Winter break: This is usually an extended time in between semesters.

Spring break: Some medical mission trips take place during medical school spring breaks.

Vacation time: During the clinical years, particularly fourth year, you may have more flexible time that you can take for vacation or other personal purposes.

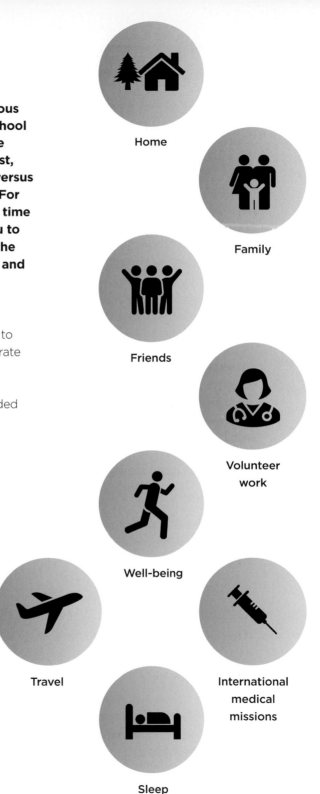

Home

Family

Friends

Volunteer work

Well-being

International medical missions

Travel

Sleep

Reflection

COMMON MYTHS

"I MUST PUBLISH RESEARCH OVER THE SUMMER OR I WILL NOT MATCH TO A RESIDENCY"

It is unlikely that what you do during the summer will make or break your residency application. Even if you do research, getting a publication is difficult and not guaranteed. Yes, research undertaken over the summer can help in certain super-competitive fields, but it is not essential. There are other times that you can do research.

"I MUST DO SOMETHING RELATED TO MEDICINE DURING THE SUMMER"

You don't have to do anything you don't want to do. You can travel (just for fun, not a medical mission), spend time with family, work in a non-health care capacity, write, and read. This is OK and may be just what you need to come back refreshed and ready to study hard again.

"SUMMER WILL BE MY LAST CHANCE TO HAVE FREE TIME— ONCE I BEGIN MY FUTURE CAREER, I'LL ALWAYS BE WORKING"

You will have other times. They may not be quite such long stretches of time, but there will be opportunities to explore side interests and develop yourself, personally and professionally.

"I MUST STUDY OVER SUMMER AND DURING BREAKS"

You can study if you want to but don't feel like you have to study. They are called breaks for a reason! Breaks are generally in between courses or exams, so there's really no need to study unless you are making up course content. Remember the importance of mind breaks for your studies and self-care for your overall well-being.

Pro tips

TALK IT THROUGH

Meet with a faculty member or dean advisor to discuss your summer plans. They are there to help guide you through your decisions and your personal and professional development throughout medical school.

"In medicine, you can always learn more, do more, give more... but you must carve out a very intentional space for you and those people and things you love. That is what makes you a better physician."

CHAPTER SIX

EXTRACURRICULARS

Besides learning the curricular content, you will have the opportunity to get involved in any number of extracurricular activities. These endeavors can be enriching and add to your personal and professional development. Your "extra" time is valuable, though, so you will want to spend it wisely. Favor quality of involvement over quantity. There's no medical school award for "Most Extracurriculars."

Some students are concerned that they do the "right" extracurriculars to help them match to a residency, but there's no must-have involvement when it comes to residency applications. Ultimately, be guided by what you are passionate about, what you want to learn about, and what you see as a potential part of your future career. Develop yourself and your interests and you can't go wrong.

This chapter covers some of the broad categories of extracurricular activities, including student organizations, clinical activities, scholarly concentration programs, and opportunities to represent your class in student government or other committees. Also included are a fourth-year student's tips for making the most of your involvement in extracurricular activities while not stretching yourself too thin, as well as what matters from a residency application standpoint. Research, an important extracurricular element for many students and closely related to scholarly concentration programs, is covered in its own chapter (see Chapter Seven).

STUDENT ORGANIZATIONS

There will be many student organizations that you can join during medical school. These can help connect you with things you love, provide meaningful service opportunities, help you in specialty exploration and professional networking, and allow opportunities for leadership on a regional and even national scale. Feel free to sample several but then commit to only the limited number that you feel will benefit you the most.

SERVICE ORGANIZATIONS

Many organizations are service-oriented and can provide you with opportunities to engage in volunteer work at your institution or in the local community. These can provide some students with meaning, particularly if service has been an important part of their lives before medical school.

SPECIALTY INTEREST GROUPS

Specialty interest groups can help students learn more about a particular specialty, meet and hear from faculty in those specialties, and explore their interests.

It's OK to be involved in a specialty interest group without being sure about your interests—it's all about learning and exploring.

IDENTITY GROUPS

These groups help students connect with peers who self-identify in similar groups (for example, by religion, ethnicity, sexuality, or minority status) and support one another.

ACADEMIC AND PROFESSIONAL GROUPS

Some student organizations are focused around student academic development and many national professional organizations, such as the American Medical Association, have local chapters. Getting involved in a local branch of a national organization can provide opportunities for students to assume regional or national leadership positions.

SOCIAL GROUPS

Other organizations are based around common interests outside of medicine, such as music, art, or athletics.

Pro tips

BE A FOUNDER

Is there no student organization that captures your passion or interest? Start one! Many student organizations are founded by students themselves. You can also resuscitate a languishing one that has lacked your energy and vision.

GETTING INVOLVED

Getting involved right at the beginning of the first semester can be challenging as you're still adapting to the new routine. Fourth-year medical student Koumudi Thingaru offers advice on making the transition a smooth one.

1 Reflect on what's important to you

Take a step back and figure out what kinds of activities you enjoy and are important to you—for example, community service, advocacy, teaching, research—and which organizations or groups at your school offer these.

2 Explore your options

Attend student organization fairs in the first semester to get an idea of what is available. It can also be helpful to think about future leadership roles within these organizations that you can see yourself in. Research opportunities may not be present at the fair, so if research is important to you, make sure you reach out to faculty members you would like to work with. Cold calls and emails may feel awkward, but they can lead to great opportunities.

3 Don't overcommit

Make sure you only sign up for activities because you can contribute to and learn from them, and not just to put them on your CV. Looking back, I would say I had two extracurricular involvements that were my proudest contributions. First, the year I became vice president of a student organization focused on teaching and using medical Spanish, my team and I worked to re-establish the dwindling interest and membership in the organization. Second, teaching sexual health classes to middle-school students in local public schools who would otherwise not have had a sexual health curriculum was extremely rewarding.

4 Know when it's time to step away

It can be hard to recognize when you have too much on your plate. Signs can be that you are missing meetings for multiple organizations and, even when you attend, you feel like you have not contributed anything significant in over a month. If you are starting to see consistent decline in exam performance because of extracurricular activities, that is a red flag to reconsider your involvement.

CLINICAL ACTIVITIES

Particularly prior to your clinical rotations, extracurricular activities can help you hone your clinical skills, participate in meaningful service, and expose you to specialties. They can help root you in why you went to medical school in the first place—which is sometimes hard to remember in the thick of lectures and exams. Note that many schools do include curricular elements during the preclinical years that allow for early clinical exposure.

SHADOWING

Some students will set up shadowing experiences that expose them to certain specialties. You typically coordinate these efforts on your own, fitting them around your schedule. While shadowing can be a useful experience, it is not necessary for you to determine your eventual specialty. See also: Shadowing, pages 80–81.

STUDENT-RUN FREE CLINICS

Student-run free clinics are common in medical schools. These offer low-cost or no-cost patient care to underserved populations. Students can assume leadership and managerial positions within these clinics with longitudinal involvement. Volunteering at these clinics can help students provide meaningful service, get to know the local community, and gain exposure to patient flow and quality improvement.

Liability issues

If you are engaging in clinical work outside of your school's curriculum, be sure to know your school's policies surrounding this and whether you are insured by your institution's malpractice coverage. Your student affairs office can assist.

OTHER VOLUNTEER ACTIVITIES

There may be other opportunities to engage in clinical volunteer work, both coordinated by your institution and/or within the local community. All can help you improve your practical skills and develop your clinical judgment. It is important that you are always working under the appropriate supervision and at a level commensurate with your training.

MEDICAL MISSIONS AND INTERNATIONAL WORK

Participating in medical missions (typically internationally) can be rewarding. See also: International Experiences, pages 78–79.

"Volunteering with a free clinic is a meaningful way to gain clinical experience and exposure to a diverse patient population."

SCHOLARLY CONCENTRATION PROGRAMS

Scholarly Concentration Programs (SCPs), offering medical students the chance to develop a focused area of scholarship, exist at a growing number of schools. Some of these programs are required and some are elective. All require commitment and work for ultimate scholarly productivity and success. If your school does not have a program, it is still possible to develop a focal area of interest and work in an aspect of medicine that you are passionate about.

SHOULD I PARTICIPATE?

This is a moot point if the program is required at your school, but if it is voluntary, you should give this some thought. A scholarly concentration (SC) may make good sense if one of the focal areas offered aligns with your particular passion or interest. Being part of an SCP can help you build a skill set and associated scholarship that you can use in your career. It may not make sense if you already have a specialized skill set from prior experiences and none of the SCs offered particularly appeal to you. Investigate the requirements thoroughly.

WHICH SC SHOULD I CHOOSE?

You may have multiple interests that you want to explore in an SCP. If you are in between two or more areas, explore what possibilities exist to bridge your interests and what currency expertise in each area could provide for your future career. A rarer SC might help differentiate you and provide more unique strengths. Ultimately, you need to choose an area because you are passionate about it and not because you think you "should" do a certain SC. Meet with a faculty or dean advisor if you need help deciding.

HOW TO SUCCEED IN AN SCP?

SCPs are designed to help students be productive in scholarship. You get what you put in. Be engaged in the material, meet all deadlines, respond to email communication in a timely manner, and always conduct yourself professionally. SCPs can connect you with role models and mentors who are doing the work you hope to do one day. Network and connect with them as well as SCP alumni. You may just find great mentors through your involvement.

"Scholarly concentration programs afford students a unique opportunity to pursue their own passions, develop into lifelong thinkers and learners, and personalize their medical school experience. Critical thinking and research skills gained through scholarly work serve students and their patients across an entire career."

Rachel Wolfson, MD, University of Chicago Pritzker Medical School

SCHOLARLY CONCENTRATION AREAS

Here are some of the most frequently offered scholarly concentration areas. If your school does not have an SCP, these areas may provide inspiration for you to develop a focal area in one of these independently.

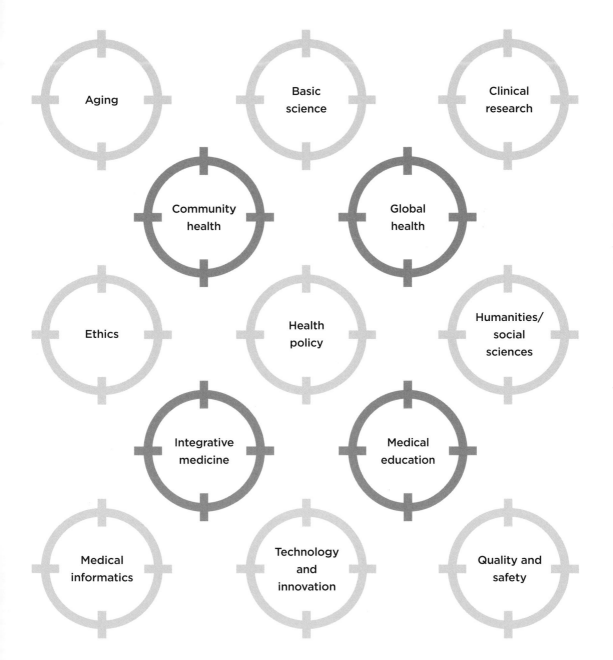

Aging

Basic science

Clinical research

Community health

Global health

Ethics

Health policy

Humanities/ social sciences

Integrative medicine

Medical education

Medical informatics

Technology and innovation

Quality and safety

STUDENT GOVERNMENT AND REPRESENTATION

Opportunities will exist for you to represent your class within student government or separately as a representative to various school committees. Leadership is a quality valued by residency program directors, as well as academic honor societies. The commitments for these roles can vary significantly and often these are elected positions or appointed by the administration. Understand the commitment, talk to older peers in these positions, and weigh your involvement carefully before putting yourself in the running.

STUDENT GOVERNMENT

Serving in student government can be great leadership experience and may involve liaising with administration and different groups on campus. Head positions like president and vice president may require a lot of time and commitment. Understand the extent of this, as you will be balancing a rigorous academic course load. You should not take on a position to pad out your resume. Take it on if you love student government and you truly want to be involved (see opposite).

> "As class president, my greatest role is that of a resource, and the trust that my classmates place in me makes the experience very rewarding. My biggest advice to someone thinking about getting involved in class leadership is to get to know your classmates! Remember that you're running for them."

Daniel Bestorous, fourth-year medical student

CURRICULAR AND COMMITTEE REPRESENTATIVES

If you are interested in medical education, serving as a curriculum representative to various school committees can expose you to behind-the-scenes educational decisions, let you get to know faculty and deans, and allow you to act as the voice of your class and potentially effect change.

HONOR COUNCIL

Students can be part of an honor council to preside over professionalism concerns and breaches of a school's honor code.

WELLNESS COMMITTEES

Many schools also have committees dedicated to student wellness with student representation.

NATIONAL REPRESENTATIVE POSITIONS

Organizations such as the AAMC have student representatives who bring school concerns to a national platform.

EXTRACURRICULARS AND RESIDENCY

Sprinkles and other decorations can't hide a poorly made cake that has a structural defect. Do not prioritize extracurriculars over academic performance.

What the sprinkles can do is personalize the cake and show who you are. Do extracurricular activities because you derive meaning from your involvement and they align with your interests.

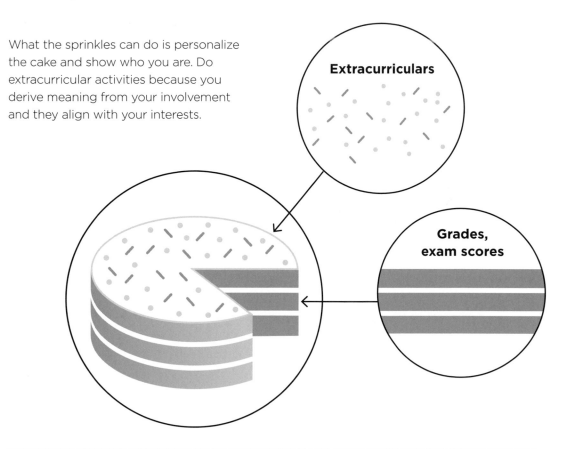

Extracurriculars

Grades, exam scores

"Focus on being the best doctor you can be, prioritizing your clinical studies to provide great patient care. Then, involve yourself with extracurricular activities that truly interest you. It is better to spend meaningful time in a few select activities—perhaps even serving in a leadership or organizational role—than to volunteer in hundreds of smaller activities."

Dr. Lisa Willett, Program Director in Internal Medicine, University of Alabama, Birmingham

CHAPTER SEVEN

RESEARCH

There is significant pressure for medical students to get involved in research, even from the very first days of medical school. Some of that pressure may come from a belief that it is a necessary box to check for residency, and then the compulsion sets in if peers start getting involved.

Pretty soon, you have full-blown research anxiety syndrome. You may find yourself thinking, "How can I get involved with research? When can I fit it in? I don't like research. But I need to be on a publication. I don't even know what specialty I will pursue!"

Deep breaths.

Getting involved in research has a lot of great benefits for medical students. You will learn about an important facet of medicine and gain skills that can help you in your future practice, regardless of whether or not you continue to do research later in your career. Like other extracurricular activities, research can be time-consuming, and you'll need to find a balance that works for you so you can continue to thrive in your studies. Research is often a positive in your residency applications, particularly in highly competitive specialties, but you can also engage in other scholarly work that provides similar benefits.

This chapter covers the basic benefits of doing research, when to do it during medical school, how to choose a project, an institutional review board (IRB) primer, and manuscript authorship.

WHY DO RESEARCH?

Many medical schools require students to undertake some kind of research or other scholarly activity at some point during their four years. But aside from having to do it, there are great reasons to want to do it too.

LEARN ABOUT THE SCIENTIFIC PROCESS

Dr. Vineet Arora, Professor of Medicine at University of Chicago, says, "There's no better way to understand the scientific process than through participating in it" (see opposite, also). This process yields new discoveries, therapies, and practice guidelines. Exploring topics that interest you will feed your intellectual curiosity and develop your problem-solving skills.

CRITICALLY APPRAISE THE LITERATURE

Being engaged in research will help you understand the strengths and limitations of research. This will help you critically appraise the literature and apply it to future patients.

RECEIVE MENTORSHIP FROM FACULTY

At the minimum, you can get to know a faculty member and their specialty better. You could also find a true mentor through the process—score! See also Chapter Eight: Finding Mentors and Being a Mentee.

DEVELOP EXCELLENT HABITS

To be successful in research requires self-discipline, goal-setting, organization, time management, focus, and teamwork.

PLAN YOUR FUTURE CAREER

Do you want research to be a part of your career? Do you want to stay in academic medicine? Do you want to become a physician-scientist? Your research experience can give you some answers. It may also strengthen your residency application (see page 104).

PRODUCE SCHOLARSHIP

If the project becomes a poster and/or publication, you will experience the joy of seeing your work published, which is always a bonus (see pages 106–107).

When should you NOT do research?

+ If you are struggling to pass your courses: Your academic work should always come first.

+ You've done it and you don't like it: Maybe you've done a lot of research prior to medical school and know it's not for you. Don't discount, though, that you might like a different kind of research.

+ You are only doing it because you believe you have to do it: You will lack the interest and motivation that are critical for success. (Note: This does not apply if you actually have to do it!)

"Even if you don't go on to become a physician-scientist, the epidemic of misinformation requires you to have foundational training in research so you can ensure your patients get the best evidence-based treatments."

CHOOSING A PROJECT

How do you know if a research project is a good fit for you? There are some important considerations to keep in mind. Note that it is always easier to join an established project or one that is being developed by a team than it is to create your own independently—this will be a lot more work and still requires you to find a faculty mentor to guide you so you don't get stuck along the way.

YOUR GOALS AND TIMELINE

Reflect on your goals and priorities for the research experience. Is your goal to get a publication from a summer project? To dabble in clinical research to see if you like it? To get to know faculty or a specialty better? Is it a school requirement? Does the project align with these goals?

RESEARCH TOPIC

Is the topic really interesting to you? Or does it make you feel "meh"? It is important to select a project that you are genuinely excited about in order to stay motivated, even if there are delays and challenges—because there are always delays and challenges.

FACULTY MENTOR

Is the faculty member known to be good to work with and approachable? Who will be your direct supervisor? Sometimes students sign up to work with a specific faculty member, but it turns out someone else (such as a resident or graduate student) will be supervising them and they have little contact with the faculty mentor. Will you get the supervision and faculty interaction you are looking for? Mentors who have a record of facilitating student scholarly output (posters, presentations, and publications) are ideal.

YOUR ROLE

What will your role be? Do you have the necessary skills? Will you have an opportunity to be an author on a publication? If this is one of your goals, be sure to know whether it is a possibility. It is OK to ask.

OVERALL COMMITMENT

Before signing up to a project, realistically assess your ability to participate fully, taking into account your curriculum and other responsibilities. Get an understanding of the project's timeline and what is expected in terms of your involvement, including during and after any planned dedicated research time.

> "In addition to the right mentor, it is important to choose a topic you are interested in and passionate about. Although your interests may change with time, this will make it easier to put in the effort to do a good job."
>
> Ramin Garmany, MD/PhD student

RESEARCH PROJECT
SPEED SCALE

Clearly, there is great variability in research, depending on the specific project, supervision, motivation, your role, the size of the research team, and phases of the moon (maybe not that last one), but here is a general scale of project speed in relation to the complexity of different types of research projects.

Literature review

Case report

Survey study

Database studies

Systematic review/meta-analysis

Retrospective chart review

Prospective cohort

Qualitative

Basic science

Randomized controlled trial

WHEN TO DO RESEARCH

While you could theoretically do research at any time, there are some periods that are more conducive to focusing on research than others, and some parts of a study will require more dedicated time than others. For instance, it takes a good deal of time up front to design a study or to perform data collection, if needed. It's best to align high-involvement research phases with dedicated research time if possible.

1 SUMMER

If you have a summer off from medical school, this is a nice block of uninterrupted time to make some research progress. If your goal is to complete a project by the end of the summer and it requires IRB approval, suss out whether the study is on track to be approved by the time you start. You could also continue helping once the school year starts, if you are in a position to balance school and the continued commitment.

2 RESEARCH ELECTIVE

Many schools offer the ability to take research electives during the clinical years and/or at various other points during the curriculum, such as peri-boards study. These vary in length but could be another valuable opportunity to dedicate time to research.

3 PRECLINCAL OR CLERKSHIP YEARS

It can be difficult to do research while entrenched in your studies, but some students have made it work by keeping their commitment manageable and flexible. Getting started and established in a study during a dedicated period helps. Be realistic when starting new studies during busy school times.

4 FOURTH YEAR

The fourth year is often much more flexible in terms of requirements and when things happen. You could carve out time to finish up projects in time for residency applications or do research during flexible times, such as interview season.

5 YEAR OFF

Some students decide to take a year off to pursue research full-time, often between years 2 and 3, or years 3 and 4. These students may be aiming to pursue competitive, research-heavy specialties or planning careers as physician-scientists. There may be fellowships or stipends available to help fund these years, but these positions are competitive.

Pro tips

FUNDING RESEARCH

Explore possible funding options through your school or professional organizations to help support your summer research or longitudinal projects.

IRBs: A medical student's primer

Institutional review boards (IRBs) may seem shrouded in mystery and intimidating to medical students. This is partly due to not knowing exactly who the IRBs are and what they do. You will likely interact with the IRB in some way during medical school if you are involved in research. Don't be afraid to reach out to ask them questions, and appreciate the vital function they have in ensuring ethical and just research practices.

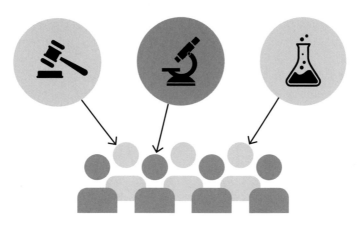

WHO: Five or more members with at least one of each—scientist, non-scientist, somebody external to the institution, subject advocate.

WHAT: Ensure that research carried out at institutions protects people being studied and follows state and federal regulations.

KEY CONCERNS: Minimization of risk, favorable risk, benefit ratios, equitable subject selection, informed consent, privacy protection, ongoing safety monitoring, and special protection for vulnerable subjects.

TYPES OF REVIEW:

+ Exempt—no collection of identifying information via surveys, retrospective research, or normal educational procedures.

+ Expedited—minimal risk studies that can be handled without the whole board (nothing high-risk, such as vulnerable populations, investigational drugs, sensitive procedures).

+ Full—everything else.

RESEARCH AND RESIDENCY APPLICATIONS

How important is research for residency applications? The short answer is that it varies. For some specialties and programs, it's not at all necessary to do research, although understanding the research process is important to practicing evidence-based medicine as a future physician. It is usually a plus on your application (as long as you can discuss it knowledgeably in an interview). However, research is secondary to academic performance and you may have other pursuits that you will want to prioritize ahead of it.

HIGHLY COMPETITIVE SPECIALTIES

For certain highly competitive specialties, research is a must, ideally in that specific specialty and with resultant presentations and publications, although any research is important experience that can be translated to other settings. Some students decide to take a research year off if they are pursuing a highly competitive specialty and want to build research in that area. Others can successfully incorporate research during their medical school studies to produce research scholarship.

OTHER SPECIALTIES

For other specialties, the value of research is variable. It can be program-specific—within any specialty, there can be programs that care more about research than others. However, other forms of scholarly work may be just as valuable if they align with your particular interests and strengths (see opposite). Research in the specialty you are applying to can indicate your interest, but it needn't be a deal breaker if it's in a different specialty—residency faculty will appreciate that you have since seen the light!

WHEN UNSURE ABOUT SPECIALTY

If you are unsure which area you want to go into and deciding on a research project, focus on either a project in the most competitive specialty you are considering or just a project that you find interesting and exciting. In residency interviews, you must be prepared to talk about any research project you have listed on your CV or application, and you'll want to do so with genuine interest and knowledge. If you are in between two specialties, you could try to find a project that relates to both, although that may be hard to come by.

Pro tips

YOUR APPLICATIONS

When applying to residency, include all significant research experiences, even if they did not result in a presentation or publication. You still gained skills and learned more about the research process—all of which are valuable.

OTHER SCHOLARLY WORK

Besides research, there are other ways to contribute knowledge to the medical community that qualify as scholarly activity. In general, scholarly activity must be work that is shared with peers and subject to peer review. Note that the ACGME, which oversees graduate medical education, requires scholarly activity by residents, leaving the definition broad for programs who may want their residents to be able to engage in population health, quality improvement, or other areas besides biomedical research.

There are a number of different types of scholarly activity beyond research:

 PERSPECTIVE PIECES/OP-EDS These are evidence-based pieces that make an argument about a current issue of interest. Many medical journals have a section for this kind of submission. In newspapers and similar publications, these are op-eds. In both kinds of writing, you are synthesizing current knowledge to make it useful and informative for readers and this may involve a call to action.

 LETTERS TO THE EDITOR Some students have published their letters to the editor of national medical journals, often in response to studies that have some link to medical students. You can share your analysis and insights in a brief (low word count) format.

 BOOK CHAPTERS Faculty members writing chapters or editing a whole book may need assistance with writing. These opportunities often come about through an existing mentor–mentee relationship.

 PUBLISHED CURRICULA OR EDUCATIONAL MODULES Interested in medical education? There are peer-reviewed sites where you can share curricula and educational modules. This is scholarship. This can also include patient education materials.

WORKSHOP TEACHING Participating in a workshop at a regional or national meeting often means helping to create faculty development content and passing peer review to be selected. This is considered "scholarship of teaching."

WHITE PAPERS AND POLICY BRIEFS For those interested in health policy, scholarly output may take the form of a white paper or policy brief. Like educational scholarship, this is unique and can make you stand out in an application crowd.

AUTHORSHIP

If you have had a successful research endeavor, hopefully you will be an author on a publication (if you meet the criteria to be a listed author). Your position on the author list depends on your role within the study. When junior in your career, first author is the most coveted position. Some faculty members will make a student or resident first author, even if the faculty member did most of the work, because they are either generous unicorns and/or they would rather not be the senior author.

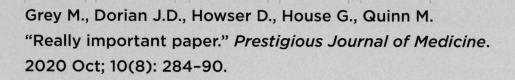

Grey M., Dorian J.D., Howser D., House G., Quinn M. "Really important paper." *Prestigious Journal of Medicine*. 2020 Oct; 10(8): 284–90.

1 **First author**—did most of the work and played a major part in writing the manuscript. Coveted position. There is such a thing as co-first authorship for people who contributed equally, with both names marked with an asterisk, although someone will still be listed first.

2 **Second author**—behind first and last authors in terms of the importance of their role on the team. Sometimes directly assisted first author if the senior author position is more in terms of title than supervisory function.

"Research skills are so important and research is something you learn by doing, regardless of what publications come out of it. That being said, as a student, be clear and honest with your mentors if one of your goals is to have your name on a publication. And if that's the case, expect to put in the work for it."

Zayna Bakizada, fourth-year medical student

Do I qualify to be an author?

You have to have been sufficiently involved throughout the study to qualify for authorship. Can you say yes to all of the following?

+ Did you contribute to the conception and design of the study and/or data analysis or interpretation?

+ Did you help draft the paper or provide critical revision?

+ Did you help with final revision of the published version?

If you haven't met all of these conditions, you may instead be listed in the acknowledgments section at the end of the paper, which lists people who were important to the study but did not fully satisfy the authorship requirements.

3 4 **Middle authors**—in order of contributions. If there are many in the middle all with similar contributions, they may be listed in alphabetical order. Sometimes, the next-to-last author is next in seniority/stature to last author. This part of the authorship list can feel arbitrary.

5 **Last author**—often the senior or supervisory person on the team, who helped the first author. Faculty members at a later stage of their careers may prefer this position to first author, as it indicates mentorship.

Pro tips

CORRESPONDING AUTHOR

The corresponding author is typically the first or last author, and this position carries certain status, too. The corresponding author will be listed as the study contact and will handle press inquiries, and so on. Often, it is the person who is submitting a paper for publication.

PART

PROFESSIONAL RELATIONSHIPS AND WELL-BEING

CHAPTER EIGHT

FINDING MENTORS AND BEING A MENTEE

The word "mentor" can conjure up an image of a wise elder who takes a young protégé under their golden wing. Mentorship has evolved over time to be less formal, to come in different forms, and even to be virtual, yet it still brings important benefits to both the mentee and the mentor.

Mentors can demystify the process of becoming a doctor, answer questions and provide advice, connect you with career opportunities and networks, and serve as a key support during the rigors of training. They may impact your choice of specialty. They may write a letter of recommendation for your residency applications. They may help you write your first research publication. They are your role models.

All physicians, on some level, went to medical school because they wanted to help people, and mentoring is a great way for faculty to feel rewarded by helping their mentees succeed. It can also benefit their careers as well as yours. Importantly, mentorship is a relationship. Just like in life, some relationships are more meaningful than others, some may be more transactional, and some were not meant to be. Approach mentorship as a relationship. Be thoughtful about who you approach. Put time and care into growing good partnerships. Move on respectfully if it's just not working out.

This chapter covers different types of mentors, how to find good mentors, and establishing and cultivating the mentor–mentee relationship so that it meets your needs and is mutually beneficial. And remember, you can always pay it forward by being a mentor for someone more junior than you.

TYPES OF MENTORS

There are many different mentorship models beyond the traditional dyad (see: The Expert below). Many schools have peer mentoring programs where you are matched with an older student. These near-peer mentors can be helpful by sharing how they have navigated the curriculum, letting you know what to expect, providing advice and recommending resources. Faculty mentors may assist with career support, research mentorship, work–life integration, specialty selection, or any number of other areas. Depending on your specific needs, you may want to utilize some or all of these mentor types during your medical school years.

THE EXPERT

Species: Esteemed faculty member
Common behaviors: Taking you under their wing, sharing opportunities, network-building, providing inspiration, being a role model
Life span: Potential for longitudinal support, throughout medical school and even beyond
Incidence: Rare. If you find one, rejoice! If not, don't despair—see below

THE PEER

Species: Older students and classmates
Common behaviors: Giving just-in-time relevant advice and support, understanding your specific needs, being a role model
Life span: Can be longitudinal or episodic
Incidence: Common—they are all around you

THE GROUP MENTOR

Species: Faculty member who is mentor to a group of peers
Common behaviors: Providing group support and advice, facilitating discussions designed to promote the group's professional development
Life span: Often longitudinal

Incidence: Many schools are set up with built-in group mentors for small groups, or they could be faculty advisors for student interest groups

THE COACH

Species: Faculty member with needed expertise
Common behaviors: Providing help around a discrete performance-based issue, such as giving presentations or improving clinical skills
Life span: Episodic, focused
Incidence: Common, may require a referral from faculty and/or deans

Pro tips

Sometimes, what you seek is a sponsor: someone with positional influence who can advocate for you and introduce you to key people and opportunities. Some mentors may also be sponsors. While mentors advise, sponsors advocate and promote.

"Good mentors invite your perspective and honestly share their own experiences and lessons learned. Mentors point you to resources and view their job as cultivating your success."

FINDING MENTORS

Medical students often share that they have trouble finding mentors—or finding good mentors. It's important to keep in mind that you can have many mentors who can help you with different parts of your journey through medical school. There are people all around you who could provide mentorship in some way.

DETERMINE WHAT YOU NEED

In what aspect of your career or life are you looking for mentorship? Is it in research around a specific project idea? Is it general professional development in your specific goal focus area? Is it for work–life integration? All of the above? Reflect on what help you hope to receive in order to best identify potential mentors who can meet those needs.

ASK FOR REFERRALS

Deans, advisors, and older peers may be able to point you to mentors who share similar interests to you or who have taken a career path that you also hope to pursue. They can suggest faculty who have a track record of helping students and are known to be good to work with.

GATHER INTEL

Did a faculty member who seems awesome give a lecture to your class? Did your school publicize a faculty member's recently published study that is right up your alley? Is a peer leading a student organization for a topic that you are passionate about? Gather some intel via internet searches, peers, and faculty to see whether this person could be a potential mentor (see box opposite).

DON'T OVERLOOK THE OBVIOUS OR NONTRADITIONAL

You may be assigned advisors, deans, and peer mentors from the beginning—sometimes these people can be excellent mentors for you. Be sure not to overlook them. In today's digitally connected society, students have also found virtual mentors from other institutions via social media. Navigating a relationship over Zoom can be challenging, but it can be done.

Pro tips

MENTOR TRAITS

You don't want a mentor who is just an older version of you. You want a mentor who can provide different strengths and perspectives to complement your own and fill in any gaps you have.

TEST THE WATERS

Once you have identified a potential mentor, ask to meet with them to talk about your career or advice they may have. Share your background and your goals. People become mentors when there is mutual respect and strong rapport. Proceed if there's chemistry. If not, there is no harm done and you will hopefully have received some helpful advice. (If they never responded to your email outreach, it's for the best.)

Signs of a good potential mentor

+ Has successful mentees

+ Is approachable

+ Answers your emails in a timely manner

+ Is known to work with students

+ Is recommended by other students

+ Has time (some successful faculty members with big responsibilities will not)

+ Makes time for you and is present with you

+ Seems sincerely interested in you as a person

+ Is someone you could see yourself becoming in the future

"Remember that you can have different mentors for different aspects of your life. You may not find everything in one mentor and that's OK; there's always room for more. Be approachable yet bold enough to ask for guidance. And most importantly, remember to stay in touch and update your mentors on your life's journey."

Ria Roberts, MD, Geriatrics Fellow
Harvard Medical School

ESTABLISHING THE
RELATIONSHIP

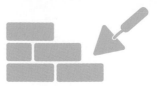

You have found a potential mentor with whom you connect well. You sense the presence of mutual respect and it feels like a good fit. What next? How exactly do you ask someone to be your mentor? This may feel daunting, perhaps similar to asking someone on a date. Just keep in mind that, unlike a date, it is not personal.

SET THE SCENE

Make sure you tell your maybe mentor why you admire and respect them.
If you haven't already shared your story, where you are headed in life, and what inspires you, now's the time.

ASK "WOULD YOU BE MY MENTOR?"

It may sound bold but this is the most direct approach. Let your mentor know what advice you are looking for and how often you hope to meet (for example, quarterly, monthly, or as needs arise). Remember that they will feel honored that you asked and if they say no it's likely because they wouldn't be able to devote the necessary time. You could also say something like, "Is it OK if we keep having these meetings?" without ever formally asking, but this could be confusing and the mentor/mentee roles may not be as defined.

FOLLOW UP

If they say yes, high five! But also know that it is up to you to take the initiative to set up future meetings and take the lead in growing the relationship. Make it easy for your mentor to help you.

The stealth mentor

Sometimes, mentoring relationships develop quietly and naturally over time without any explicit agreements. One day, you just find yourself referring to the faculty member as your mentor to your friends and family. This may stem from an existing relationship—someone who you were assigned to work with or similar—but if it happens, go with it. Consider making the relationship more explicit by discussing the evolving mentoring relationship together. The more explicit the mentoring process is, the more active and intentional it becomes.

ROLES AND RESPONSIBILITIES

These are general roles and responsibilities for mentors and mentees, but your specific mentoring situation may have unique elements, so use this as a rough guide for expectations.

Mentor

+ Helps mentee set educational/career goals
+ Provides encouragement
+ Serves as a positive role model
+ Assists mentee in thinking through difficult decisions
+ Shares expertise
+ Gives honest and constructive feedback
+ Celebrates mentee achievements
+ Responds to outreach by mentee in a timely manner
+ Connects mentee to opportunities

Both

+ Maintain mutual respect and trust
+ Maintain confidentiality
+ Attend all scheduled meetings
+ Listen actively

Mentee

+ Takes the lead in setting up meetings and growing the relationship
+ Respects the mentor's time
+ Seeks guidance and advice in their professional development
+ Assumes responsibility for their own decisions and actions
+ Openly shares successes and failures
+ Receives feedback well
+ Sets goals with the help of their mentor
+ Follows through on commitments
+ Updates their mentor with progress over time

CULTIVATING THE RELATIONSHIP

Once a mentor–mentee relationship has been established, the mentee will need to manage it actively, in order to ensure that the relationship is as successful as possible and yields the desired outcomes. The mentee takes ownership of the relationship and directs information flow. This is called "managing up."

SET UP MEETINGS

After agreeing on a meeting frequency, set up meetings based on your mentor's preferences for meeting—by phone or video call, or in person. Set an agenda beforehand to organize the time efficiently. You may share the agenda ahead of time or just refer to it for your own planning and notes.

USE DIRECT COMMUNICATION

Directly express your needs. Directly address conflicts such as paper authorship or areas where you are unsure about something. Tailor communication based on your mentor's preferences for information, such as sending information ahead of time for them to review before a meeting. If unclear about how they would like you to communicate, ask.

TAKE RESPONSIBILITY

After you have set a timeline, with your mentor's input, stick to it and take responsibility for achieving goals. If you make errors (who doesn't?) or miss deadlines, take ownership of this and make plans to get back on track.

KNOW YOURSELF AND YOUR MENTOR

You will need to understand your and your mentor's styles, preferences, and expectations for interaction to best navigate the relationship. This means being a good observer and picking up on cues.

RESPECT YOUR MENTOR'S TIME

Your mentor is busy and time spent together should be focused on addressing your needs. If you haven't progressed in your work as you expected, it may be worth delaying a scheduled meeting. Have reasonable expectations for turnaround time on reviewing your work, but do clearly communicate any time-sensitive deadlines.

ANATOMY OF A GOOD MENTEE

It takes two to make a productive and mutually satisfying mentor–mentee relationship, but here's how to be a good mentee on your end. Engaging in these behaviors will make it a joy to mentor you.

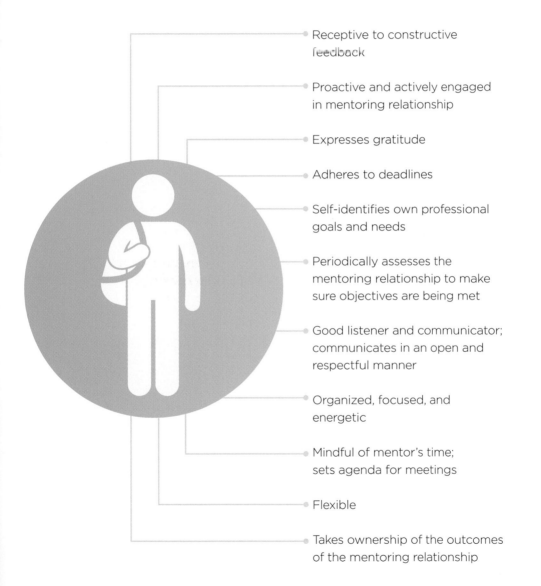

Receptive to constructive feedback

Proactive and actively engaged in mentoring relationship

Expresses gratitude

Adheres to deadlines

Self-identifies own professional goals and needs

Periodically assesses the mentoring relationship to make sure objectives are being met

Good listener and communicator; communicates in an open and respectful manner

Organized, focused, and energetic

Mindful of mentor's time; sets agenda for meetings

Flexible

Takes ownership of the outcomes of the mentoring relationship

CHAPTER NINE

OPTIMIZING WELL-BEING FOR MEDICAL SCHOOL SUCCESS

This chapter is arguably the most important one in the book. Your well-being as a medical student will shape how you learn, how you are able to manage the stresses of medical school, and your ability to find purpose and meaning in what you do.

You can't realize your full potential as a medical student and future doctor without a strong foundation of wellness that you continually build upon.

Well-being is not a static state. It is not inherited through your genes or predetermined by your past experiences. We are all in a constant state of flux with our own personal well-being. We may encounter illness, setbacks, and challenges that test our ability to maintain our well-being. Just as we use metacognition to plan, monitor, and assess our learning strategies, we can do the same for our well-being. We can assess the areas of wellness where we have strengths and the areas we need to improve upon and make the necessary adjustments toward becoming a more fully actualized and healthy individual.

While your medical school will often have well-being curricula and resources to help you maintain and improve your well-being, it is largely up to you how much you invest in this process. Engage the necessary attention, energy, and care for optimizing your own well-being to set yourself up for success in medical school. Know that you are never alone and never hesitate to seek help when you need it.

DIMENSIONS OF WELLNESS

Wellness is multidimensional. It is the interplay of many different aspects of one's life. We often think of wellness with a narrower view—being physically active or the absence of mental illness, but it's much more complex than that. The "eight dimensions of wellness" model is a useful way to explore your own well-being. Which spheres are most developed for you? Which spheres do you need to work on? Use the inventory opposite to help.

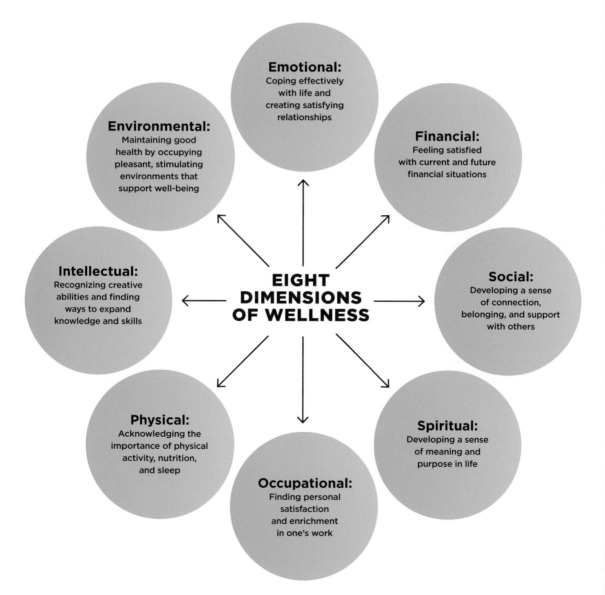

EIGHT DIMENSIONS OF WELLNESS

Emotional: Coping effectively with life and creating satisfying relationships

Financial: Feeling satisfied with current and future financial situations

Social: Developing a sense of connection, belonging, and support with others

Spiritual: Developing a sense of meaning and purpose in life

Occupational: Finding personal satisfaction and enrichment in one's work

Physical: Acknowledging the importance of physical activity, nutrition, and sleep

Intellectual: Recognizing creative abilities and finding ways to expand knowledge and skills

Environmental: Maintaining good health by occupying pleasant, stimulating environments that support well-being

Emotional
- [ ] I accept responsibility for my actions.
- [ ] I can recognize and express my feelings.
- [ ] I can cope with stress.
- [ ] I have considerable control over my life.
- [ ] I see challenges as opportunities for growth.
- [ ] I feel good about myself.
- [ ] I can learn from my mistakes.
- [ ] I can laugh at myself and life.

Financial
- [ ] I pay my bills on time.
- [ ] I have the money to meet my basic needs.
- [ ] I have a basic understanding of finances.
- [ ] I have reserves to weather unexpected expenses.
- [ ] I know who to turn to for financial questions.
- [ ] I am comfortable with how I will finance school.
- [ ] I do not carry credit card debt.

Social
- [ ] I regularly spend time with people I like.
- [ ] I balance my own needs with the needs of others.
- [ ] I have a network of friends and/or family.
- [ ] I help others and causes I believe in, when I can.
- [ ] I feel connected to my community.
- [ ] I am interested in others, including those different than me.

Spiritual
- [ ] I use my personal values and beliefs to guide my choices in life.
- [ ] I feel purpose and meaning in my life.
- [ ] I regularly use prayer, meditation, or reflection.
- [ ] I try to learn about others' beliefs and values.
- [ ] I feel gratitude for the good things in my life.
- [ ] I have optimism and faith in the future.

Occupational
- [ ] I am glad to be in medical school.
- [ ] I am productive most days in school.
- [ ] I have satisfaction and stimulation in my work.
- [ ] Medicine allows me to make good use of my talents.
- [ ] I engage in work that is meaningful.
- [ ] I have identified possible career paths in medicine that excite me.

Physical
- [ ] I regularly exercise at least three times a week.
- [ ] I get enough sleep each night.
- [ ] I eat a healthy diet.
- [ ] I get routine care for my medical issues.
- [ ] I use stress management techniques (see Stress Management, pages 124–125).
- [ ] I avoid tobacco and other substances of misuse.

Intellectual
- [ ] I try to see multiple sides of an issue.
- [ ] I try to keep up with current affairs.
- [ ] I make an effort to learn new things outside of medicine.
- [ ] I engage in intellectual discussions.
- [ ] I expose myself to creative arts performances.
- [ ] I practice skills and talents that I have (music, sports, arts, etc.).

Environmental
- [ ] I make use of fresh air, natural light, and live plants.
- [ ] I regularly clean and tidy my home.
- [ ] I set aside time to enjoy nature.
- [ ] I feel safe in my neighborhood and where I live.
- [ ] I recycle and try to conserve energy.

STRESS MANAGEMENT

Stress invokes the fight-or-flight physiologic response, which is great for escaping predators in the wild, but less helpful in medical school when maintained at high levels. Some stress is useful—it can motivate you and even help you learn. However, when stress gets out of hand, it becomes counterproductive and can have serious short-term and long-term physical and mental health consequences. Monitor your stress levels and build the following active stress-management strategies into your routine.

EXERCISE REGULARLY

Exercise is a great stress reliever. Make it a regular part of your routine, and do not skip it when exams are approaching.

ATTEND TO YOUR SOCIAL WELLNESS

Regularly carve out some quality time with people you care about, even if it's just coffee or a brief video call.

CRACK A JOKE

Humor activates, then dampens, your stress response. Incorporate things and people that make you laugh into your daily routines and downtime.

ENGAGE IN HOBBIES YOU LOVE

Find time to do the hobbies you had prior to medical school (or new ones), to help center you and calm your stress response.

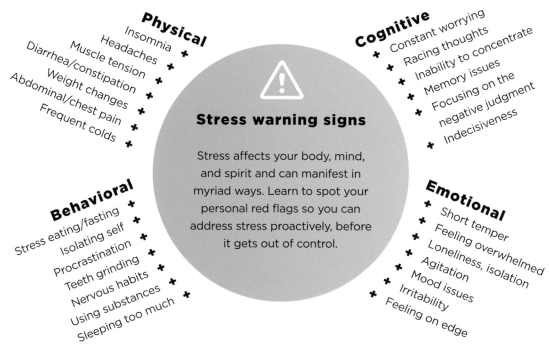

Stress warning signs

Stress affects your body, mind, and spirit and can manifest in myriad ways. Learn to spot your personal red flags so you can address stress proactively, before it gets out of control.

Physical
+ Insomnia
+ Headaches
+ Muscle tension
+ Diarrhea/constipation
+ Weight changes
+ Abdominal/chest pain
+ Frequent colds

Cognitive
+ Constant worrying
+ Racing thoughts
+ Inability to concentrate
+ Memory issues
+ Focusing on the negative judgment
+ Indecisiveness

Behavioral
+ Stress eating/fasting
+ Isolating self
+ Procrastination
+ Teeth grinding
+ Nervous habits
+ Using substances
+ Sleeping too much

Emotional
+ Short temper
+ Feeling overwhelmed
+ Loneliness, isolation
+ Agitation
+ Mood issues
+ Irritability
+ Feeling on edge

THE RELAXATION RESPONSE

The relaxation response is the opposite of the stress response. There are several techniques for invoking it, including deep abdominal breathing and body scanning, yoga, tai chi, meditation, guided imagery, and repetitive prayer. A common thread is mindfulness—being fully present in the moment without judgment or overreaction. When you are mindful, you are in the state of "being" instead of "doing." Such practices don't need to take a lot of time—even 5 or 10 minutes a day can be helpful. Consistency is key. Try the techniques below to see what works for you.

Abdominal breathing

In the stress response, we use shallow, upper-chest breathing. We can reduce the stress response by consciously performing deep abdominal breathing.

+ Get into position. Sit comfortably in a quiet, relaxed environment.

+ Place one hand on your chest and the other on your abdomen, just under your ribs. Notice how they move while you breathe.

+ Focus on your breath. Gently breathe in through your nose. Your upper chest should be still. Breathe out through pursed lips.

+ With each breath, let tension in your body dissipate. Keep breathing slowly and quietly.

+ Conclude. When you are done, notice how you feel overall.

Body scan meditation

This form of meditation has been shown to decrease cortisol levels and help with anxiety.

+ Get into position. Sit comfortably in a quiet, relaxed environment. (You can also do this lying down.) Gently close your eyes.

+ Focus on how your body feels overall. Feel the weight of your body on the chair or the floor. Take some deep breaths.

+ Starting from your feet and moving up through the body to the top of your head, focus on each part and notice how it feels. Is it tense? Painful? Relaxed? No judgment, just noticing.

+ When your attention wanders (and it will), gently bring it back to the body scan and continue.

+ Conclude. When you are done, notice how your body feels overall again. Take a few deep breaths. Gently open your eyes.

BURNOUT

Burnout is unfortunately common in physicians and medical students. It is a state of physical, emotional, and psychological exhaustion and mental distress caused by excessive professional stress. Medical students who suffer from burnout tend to have less empathy, struggle academically, and have lapses in professionalism. It can negatively affect physical and mental health and results in an unsustainable state.

COMPONENTS OF BURNOUT

 Emotional exhaustion: feelings of energy depletion or exhaustion

 Depersonalization: increased mental distance from job; cynicism

Personal accomplishment: reduced professional efficacy

"**Avoid a strategy of delayed gratification. That is, take the time now to do something outside of medicine that brings you joy. Doing so will serve you well in the long run.**"

Liselotte Dyrbye, MD, MHPE, Mayo Clinic

Risk factors

+ Unmitigated stress

+ Poor sleep, diet

+ Low levels of physical activity

+ Work-life imbalance

+ Lack of control of schedules, assignments, resources

+ Lack of social support

+ Low school attendance (increasing during school)

Burnout prevention

+ Active stress management

+ Sleep and eat well

+ Regular exercise

+ Balance work with play

+ Focus on what you can control; control attitude

+ Build and invest in your social support system

"Make an active and conscious effort to prevent burnout before it sets in, beginning in (or even before) your first year."

OPTIMIZING YOUR SLEEP

It's easy to shortchange yourself on sleep—it seems like an expendable activity in the face of looming exams and a relentless study schedule. However, not getting enough consistent restful sleep results in problems with attention, memory, and mood, and is associated with lower academic performance in college students. In terms of wellness, sleep has important roles in helping us maintain our emotional and physical well-being.

GET THE RIGHT AMOUNT OF SLEEP

In general, you should aim for 7–9 hours of sleep per night. The optimal amount varies by individual. How much sleep do you need in order to maintain your highest productivity, energy levels, and mood?

MAKE YOUR BEDROOM A SLEEP HAVEN

Your bed and bedroom should beckon slumber—invest in a quality mattress, pillows, bedding, sound machine, blackout curtains—whatever you need for a comfortable, quiet, peaceful environment. Adjust the temperature, if possible, for a cool room around 65ºF.

SET A SLEEP SCHEDULE AND STICK TO IT

Pick a consistent wake up time for weekdays AND weekends to establish a healthy sleep routine. Don't nap too late in the day. If you need to change your sleep schedule, do so gradually over time, aiming for a difference of 1–2 hours per night.

ESTABLISH AN EFFECTIVE PRE-BED ROUTINE

How you settle yourself in prior to going to bed can have a big effect on your ability to fall asleep easily. Stop studying, disconnect from devices, dim the lights, and wind down for at least 30 minutes doing something relaxing—pleasure reading, meditating, listening to music, or other relaxation response activities.

Pro tips

SEEK HELP FOR SLEEP PROBLEMS

If you have issues with sleepiness during the day, despite adequate duration of sleep at night, other potential medical issues that may be interfering with good-quality sleep, or insomnia despite implementing sleep hygiene tips, see a doctor. Since sleep affects so many facets of our well-being and learning, don't let these issues go unaddressed for too long.

☀ PROMOTE GOOD SLEEP DURING THE DAY

Expose yourself to natural light early in the day. Exercise (but not late in the evening, which can rev you up too much). Avoid alcohol, caffeine, and large meals late at night. Don't use your bed for other tasks, such as studying.

TAKE THE RIGHT ACTIONS IF YOU CAN'T SLEEP

Avoid staring at the clock or taking out your phone to catch up on emails and social media. The blue light at night can powerfully suppress melatonin. Try relaxation response activities and focus on relaxing, not sleeping. If it's been 20 minutes, get out of bed and read or do something else relaxing and try again.

THE IDEAL NAP

Napping during the day can help you maintain your productivity in the face of sleepiness. It can even improve learning and aid in laying down memories. Don't fight the nap! Have zero guilt about this.

SET THE STAGE

Select a cool, dark, quiet place to take your nap. Don't nap too late in the day or it will interfere with you falling asleep at night. Aim for between 1pm and 4pm.

Get your mind ready to nap. Set an intention for the nap, set worries aside, and use relaxation techniques if needed.

CHOOSE YOUR NAP

The power nap:
Set your alarm for 10–20 minutes. Great for study session breaks. Enough for recovery, but no grogginess.

The short-term nap:
Set your alarm for 40–60 minutes. Can help consolidate memory. May feel a little groggy upon waking.

The REM nap:
Set your alarm for 90 minutes to fulfill a full sleep cycle. Can help with creativity and learning procedural skills. Best for weekends.

THRIVING WITH A CHRONIC ILLNESS

Many students have managed a chronic illness during medical school and thrived, thanks to the support of those around them. Put your health first and know that your personal experience will help you be a better doctor in the future.

✓ ESTABLISH GOOD LOCAL CARE

If you have a chronic illness and are under the regular care of a provider, be sure to establish good care if you relocate to a new city for medical school. Having convenient, accessible care is important. If the illness begins in medical school, find a provider you like and trust. Your dean's office might be able to help make recommendations.

✓ HAVE THE RIGHT INSURANCE

All medical schools require students to have health insurance and will offer school-sponsored insurance plans for students to purchase. Be sure to know the details of the school-sponsored health insurance. You should have the option of selecting your own personal policy, provided comparable (or better) coverage.

✓ BE OPEN

Properly attending to your health conditions means regular provider visits that could conflict with classes and rotations. Being open about your illness with supportive deans, faculty, and peers can help keep you on track and connect you with important resources. Ask your dean's office to refer you to disability support services if you require any accommodations.

✓ SEEK SUPPORT FROM OTHERS

One benefit of being open is that you can find a support group of others going through similar experiences. There may be a student organization already that supports students with chronic illnesses—or you could start one.

✓ SEEK HELP WHEN NEEDED

Most important is to seek help when you need it. Your health—physical and mental—is the #1 priority.

Mental health issues

Mental health conditions such as depression and anxiety are common in medical school, yet many affected students do not seek help.

Mental health issues are normal, treatable, and critically important to address for your learning and your well-being. As a future physician, attend to your mental health needs as you would any medical condition.

Tap into your school's mental health resources: many offer counseling, dedicated providers, hotlines, and support groups.

SUBSTANCE MISUSE

Medical school is the time to retire any substance misuse that may have started prior to attending. Medical students who use drugs or drink excessive amounts of alcohol end up experiencing personal and academic consequences such as violence, suicidal ideation, cognitive impairment, and driving under the influence. It can precipitate lapses in professionalism, endanger the lives of the student and peers, and place students at risk for developing habitual use as future physicians.

X ALCOHOL

Binge drinking (defined as four or more drinks in women and five or more drinks in men in a 2-hour episode) is the most common pattern of excessive alcohol use, is most prevalent in young adults, and results in impaired verbal learning.

X MARIJUANA

Marijuana use impairs learning abilities and memory formation and is linked to depression and anxiety. Chronic use results in reduced intellectual functioning, even during periods of abstinence. While people seem to recover their cognitive abilities after quitting, when started during adolescence, it can cause long-term changes in the adult brain.

X NONMEDICAL USE OF STIMULANTS

Some students misuse stimulants such as Ritalin and Adderall in order to help them focus, believing it can help them with their academic performance. There are no studies to support this belief, and misuse can have serious adverse health effects. In a field that requires lifelong learning, stimulant misuse only serves as a temporary crutch.

X OTHER ILLEGAL DRUGS

Habit-forming illegal drug use is destructive and not compatible with a career in medicine. There are resources in every medical school to help students who need it.

Drug screens

+ Routine drug screens are performed at various points during medical school, prior to starting residency, and can be regularly or randomly performed throughout your career.

+ Testing positive for an illegal substance (or even legal in the case of certain jurisdictions and marijuana) can result in professional ramifications and employment termination.

CHAPTER TEN

CULTIVATING RESILIENCE

You likely know someone who has faced enormous adversity and was able to overcome and even grow from it. What was it about this person—maybe it was you—that allowed them to persevere, stay hopeful, learn, and move forward with grace and grit?

Resilience and well-being are related but distinct concepts. Positive well-being contributes to a person's resilience but other factors also play a role in how we are able to recover and move forward following setbacks. In medicine, having a high level of resilience not only protects us from stressors, but allows us to feel capable in the face of uncertainty, something physicians are often called upon to do. Highly resilient individuals also develop grit, stay inspired, and find meaning in their work, while staying flexible and mentally strong despite change and challenges. Clearly, then, it's important enough to be considered here.

While there's no single agreed set of components that make up resilience, much work has been done to identify associated factors, to measure resilience, and to look at how it can be cultivated. The great news is that your capacity for resilience can grow. From each setback you face, learn and grow your resilience—that is the secret sauce for thriving in medicine and in life.

WHAT IS RESILIENCE?

Resilience is the ability to bounce back from adversity, trauma, and stressful situations. It is a critical quality for medical students and physicians. Medical training is intense: medical students experience burnout and mental health issues such as depression and anxiety at a higher rate than age-matched controls. Similarly, many physicians will experience burnout and may also struggle with depression and anxiety. Resilience can be protective against the development of these issues—so cultivating resilience is an important investment of your time and energy.

WHAT IS RESILIENCE NOT?

Resilience is not immunity from stress or discomfort. Nor is it avoidance of stress. A resilient individual can experience profound distress but has a more adaptive response to it, resulting in recovery and personal growth.

Resilience *(noun)*
The capacity to recover quickly from difficulties; toughness.
(Oxford English Dictionary)

Past resilience inventory

Think about stressful or traumatic experiences you have had and consider the following:

+ How was I affected by the experience?

+ What helped me the most during that time?

+ Who did I reach out to for support?

+ What was less helpful in my response?

+ How did I overcome the challenge?

+ What did I learn about myself during the process?

+ How would I guide a friend through a similar experience?

+ Overall, what kinds of events have caused me the most distress?

The resilience well

One way to think about resilience is as a well with a reservoir of water that you are continually refreshing and drawing from. Depletion can lead to burnout and other mental health issues. The more replete the well, the better you can cope with any setbacks that come your way. Note that this is a dynamic, complex process.

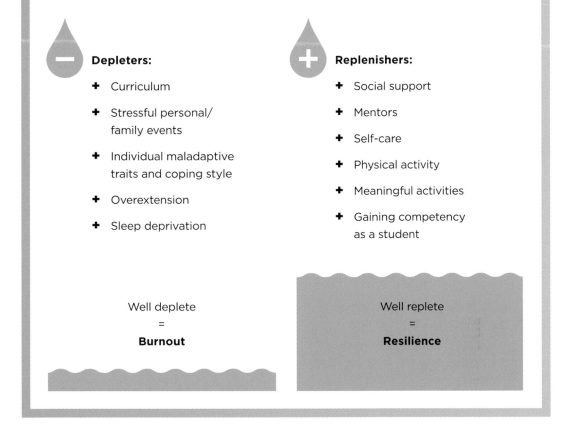

Depleters:

+ Curriculum

+ Stressful personal/ family events

+ Individual maladaptive traits and coping style

+ Overextension

+ Sleep deprivation

Replenishers:

+ Social support

+ Mentors

+ Self-care

+ Physical activity

+ Meaningful activities

+ Gaining competency as a student

Well deplete
=
Burnout

Well replete
=
Resilience

CAN YOU DEVELOP RESILIENCE?

Resilience is not an intrinsic personality trait. You can develop resilience just as you can develop your clinical reasoning skills, but it requires self-awareness and intentionality. Commit to the behaviors and strategies that contribute to resilience, as outlined on the following pages.

WHAT CAN YOU LEARN FROM YOUR PAST?

Your handling of prior stressful experiences can provide insight into your strengths and will highlight areas upon which you can build. See the box opposite to help you assess your past reactions.

STRATEGIES FOR BUILDING RESILIENCE

Many strategies can help you build resilience. They include behaviors and ways of thinking. When reflecting on your past experiences of dealing with adversity, identify the processes that resonate with and work for you. Develop your own personal strategy for making sure that your resilience well is full and regularly checked.

THINGS YOU CAN DO

PRIORITIZE SOCIAL CONNECTIONS

A key part of resilience is social connection. Prioritize your relationships and be sure not to isolate yourself when you are going through challenges. Family, friends, loved ones, and trusted mentors can all contribute to your social support circle. Find resilient role models and learn from them.

MAKE TIME FOR INTERESTS OUTSIDE OF MEDICINE

Remember the hobbies you loved prior to medical school? Don't lose those. Or explore new interests that are non-work-related. These can refresh you and provide important mental breaks.

PRACTICE MINDFULNESS

Being mindful—staying focused on the present moment in a nonjudgmental way—leads to improved well-being and decreased stress. Higher mindfulness has been linked to higher resilience.

ENGAGE IN SELF-CARE

Practice self-care in terms of your nutrition, hydration, sleep, and exercise. Be attuned to your well-being and when you need downtime. Avoid harmful substances that can temporarily mask stress but are ultimately destructive.

BE PHYSICALLY ACTIVE

We know that exercise is good for learning, improves mood and sleep, and builds resilience to stress. It also reduces the risk for developing dementia, anxiety, and depression. Exercise outdoors, in a natural environment, for an extra boost.

SET REALISTIC GOALS

Setting regular, realistic goals can make big tasks manageable and contribute to your sense of self-efficacy. Be proactive and take charge of the situation.

FIND PURPOSE AND MEANING

Participate in activities that give you a sense of purpose, meaning, and moral compass. This may be practicing a religion or volunteering in your community. Be part of something bigger than yourself.

PRACTICE GRATITUDE

At the end of the day, think about or say the things you are grateful for. Write a text or email to someone to express your gratitude.

SEEK HELP

If you need help, seek it. Asking for help is part of self-awareness and being resilient. Consider talking to a mentor or friend. A counselor or therapist can help if you feel stuck. Seeking help when you need it is a strength, not a weakness.

"Resilience can easily become another thing at which to fail. I have long since let go of trying to 'be resilient' or perfect myself. Instead, I try only to perfect my love. Love for life, for others, and the tallest order of all, for myself."

Chantal Young, PhD, Director of Medical Student Wellness, Keck School of Medicine

WAYS YOU CAN THINK

MAINTAIN PERSPECTIVE

Step back and appreciate the broader context of this event, both for you and in the wider world. It may help to talk to older peers, friends outside of medicine, family members, or mentors. Learn to recognize if you begin catastrophizing and imagining a doomed future based on this one single event.

HARNESS A GROWTH MINDSET

We first talked about the importance of a growth mindset back in Part 1 (see page 27). For those viewing themselves with a fixed mindset, a setback such as a disappointing exam score can be devastating. They think this means they are not actually "smart," or special, as they believe potential is innate. Yet to those with a growth mindset, how "smart" they are is down to them—they believe potential is developed and can be achieved through effort and acquired skills. Failure may hurt, but it is recoverable.

STAY POSITIVE

See yourself as the capable person you are—after all, you got into medical school! Keep an optimistic outlook and visualize what you want for the future. See the positive aspects of an event and let that take up space, instead of letting the negative aspects eclipse everything else.

ACCEPT CHANGE

Change happens. Your trajectory may change based on an adverse event. Instead of spending time lamenting, withdrawing from, or resisting something that can't be changed, consider how you can respond to move forward. Remember that even if you can't change the event, you can change how you respond to it.

CHAPTER ELEVEN

RELATIONSHIPS DURING MEDICAL SCHOOL

Your life will not be on hold during medical school. While you will be undergoing the academic, professional, and personal development of becoming a future physician, life goes on. Your social development, too, continues, and medical school is an important time to attend to your social spheres for support and meaning.

Coming into medical school, you likely have special people in your life—family members, close friends, and significant others. These people may have supported you in your dreams to pursue a medical career. Yet, it can sometimes be a challenge to maintain relationships during medical school due to factors like time, busyness, intensity, and schedules.

New special people will also enter into your life during medical school. You may meet your new best friend(s) or your life partner, either within or outside of school. Or, you may already have a partner and are thinking of starting a family. While in medical school, navigating your social and family lives often requires intentionality and attention. However, these important relationships also bring tremendous reward and strength that allow you to ride the ups and downs of school with grace and resilience.

This chapter explores ways of building and maintaining this very important aspect of your life. It includes knowing your social support network, maintaining friendships, and having a significant other. There are tips on managing a long-distance relationship, navigating a pregnancy, and being a parent during medical school.

In 20, 30, 40, 50 years . . . it will be about the people.

KNOW YOUR SOCIAL SUPPORT SYSTEM

Having good social support is key to thriving in medical school. Whether you start out with a little or a lot of support, you can work to build and maintain key relationships during medical school for social wellness, prevention of burnout, and making the journey to your medical degree that much more meaningful and enjoyable.

THE (EXISTING) INNER CIRCLE

Your family, partner, and closest friends will typically make up your inner circle (see opposite). These are your rocks, and you should keep as close to them as you can. It may mean scheduling calls or talking on the way to school—just keep those connections burning brightly. Some will not understand what you are going through; try not to get frustrated or impatient. Practice giving "layman's" updates about what you are doing in school and let your inner circle ground you.

NEW MEDICAL SCHOOL RELATIONSHIPS

Developing close friendships at medical school can be a tremendous source of support—people who understand the experiences that are hard to grasp for those who aren't in medical school. Some of these new relationships may add to your inner circle of support. Some shy away from dating people in the same class since a breakup means having potentially to interact with that person for many more years. Others find their life partners.

> ### Pro tips 👍
>
> ### INNER CIRCLE STRENGTH
>
> Developing and maintaining relationships takes energy and conscious thought. Friendships (and other intimate relationships) that aren't actively maintained are likely to fade away. Prioritize your inner circle, as this will help fuel you through medical school.

NEW EXTERNAL RELATIONSHIPS

In a new city, you may develop some new relationships that can be important sources of support, such as housemates, new nonmedical school friends, and the like. Medical school is like a bubble and it's easy to lose valuable perspective without outside interactions.

Circles of support

Your circles of support include your biggest fans and closest confidants, as well as the volunteer organizations you participate in, and even your ride-share driver. Think about where your relationships fall and know you are enveloped in support on many levels.

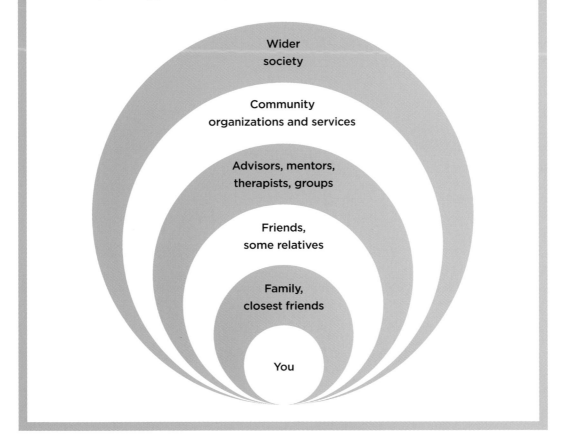

Wider society

Community organizations and services

Advisors, mentors, therapists, groups

Friends, some relatives

Family, closest friends

You

PEOPLE WHOSE JOB IT IS TO SUPPORT YOU

Such people exist! These are advisors, deans, and medical education faculty who want to support you in your pursuits. There are psychologists, therapists, and physicians. Be sure to make use of what you need to feel supported in your journey.

COMMUNITY ENGAGEMENT

Religious organizations, volunteer organizations, and other community services may also provide you with much-needed support. Engage in your community as an active member and aim to feel rooted there.

MAINTAINING FRIENDSHIPS

Long-term friendships are at risk during medical school, but they are important to our social wellness, critical for our support, and help us have more satisfying lives. Maintaining friendships while busy can be challenging. It takes attention and intentionality. Note, you may not choose to keep all of your prior friendships, which is OK. Certainly, toxic ones can go. But make the time and energy for those friendships that mean the most to you.

MULTITASK

Spend time with friends while doing things you need to do anyway, either in person or virtually. Have a call while going for a walk or commuting to school or the store. Exercise together. Go the library and do work/study in parallel. There doesn't have to be an elaborate hangout plan.

COMMUNICATE OPENLY

Make sure your friends understand your schedule and that you wish you could spend more time together—let them know this is not about avoidance or rejection.

DO MORE THAN TEXT

Texts are easy and let the other person know you are thinking about them, but ultimately they may not sustain the friendship without other more meaningful connections. Even a voicemail message is something more personal.

HANG OUT IN A GROUP

This is an efficient way to hang out with friends, and it's great when friends from different groups end up meshing well with each other. Carve out 1:1 time with friends during these times as well, for more meaningful reconnection.

SCHEDULE SOMETHING

List social needs in your calendar along with your other to-dos. Better yet, buy tickets or pay upfront for something for you and a friend so you'll be less likely to back out last minute. Also, make sure important dates like birthdays are in your calendar.

PLAN SOMETHING BIGGER

Maybe you can't get together in person during the school year, but perhaps you can plan a vacation together during a break or a weekend getaway.

BE THERE IN HARD TIMES

Does a good friend need help? Be there for them, just as you would want them to be there for you if roles were reversed.

TAKE THE TEMPERATURE

Every so often, take the temperature of your friendships. Are you satisfied with their status or do you need to prioritize certain ones that are on life support?

WHEN YOU HAVE A PARTNER

Having a significant other while attending medical school can be a great source of support and can also normalize the experience of being there. Like maintaining your close friend relationships, intentionality is necessary to keeping your relationship healthy and mutually satisfying. Some key elements can help your relationship thrive.

COMMUNICATION

Good communication is integral to any relationship, particularly when one partner is in medical school. There needs to be open, honest communication when things aren't working. Periodically check in with one another to see how both of you are feeling about your relationship.

COMMON GOALS

Together, both partners should share a common vision about their future together and work through the bumps of medical school to get there.

EXPECTATIONS

If the relationship started before medical school, there needs to be an understanding that things will be different. Time spent together will likely not be the same. Both of you will need to make compromises.

QUALITY TIME TOGETHER

Since time is so limited, time together should be marked off and protected—turn off phones, notifications (when not on call) and fully enjoy the presence of one another.

EMPATHY, SENSITIVITY

Those medical school parties can be torturous for partners who aren't in medical school, and it's easy to feel left out. Be sensitive to your partner's perspective. Your partner, too, should try to understand your lack of control over many aspects of your schedule, work, and so on.

FLEXIBILITY

Be flexible and roll with day-to-day disruptions to your plans. Medical school is only for a finite time. Still, flexibility and patience will be rewarded eventually!

Pro tips

NONMEDICAL PARTNERS

For partners not in the medical field, connecting with the significant others of other medical students can help them feel supported. Being a partner of a medical student can sometimes feel isolating, lonely, and frustrating. Some schools have support groups for significant others; there are also social media avenues to connect with other partners online.

THE LONG-DISTANCE RELATIONSHIP

Laura Upton, a fourth-year medical student at Georgetown University, started medical school when her husband started his fellowship in a distant state. Here are Laura's tips on dealing with the challenges they faced living apart for two years.

1 Adapt how you connect
Find ways to connect virtually, such as reading the same book or exercising together with the webcam on. On "Zoom nights," we kept Zoom on while studying: we would be doing our own thing, but together.

2 Communicate effectively
Be open, honest, and understanding with each other. If something isn't working for you, let your partner know. And communicate often: Tell your partner via texts you're thinking of them, send them an email or letter in the mail, or leave voicemails that will make them smile. The small things will go a long way.

3 Know each other's schedules
Doing so is critical not only for coordinating time to talk by phone or video chat, but also to feel connected day-to-day. This is especially effective if you can connect with the intricacies of each other's daily routines early on by visiting each other and experiencing firsthand the places and people in each other's lives.

4 Plan and prioritize reunions
Do this as much as your schedule and budget allow. Give yourselves permission to embrace "the ordinary" when visiting each other: Don't feel pressure to go out on fancy dates or sightsee. When parting, have the next trip planned. Knowing when you will be together again helps make the days apart more tolerable.

5 Embrace the challenge
You cannot have growth without challenge—so, the faster you learn to embrace it as a couple, the more you will grow together. If you can get through separation, your relationship will be stronger and more resilient than ever.

PREGNANCY DURING MEDICAL SCHOOL

Deciding to have a child during medical school is a big decision. Approach it with planning and forethought. Who will be your support system? What resources are available to you? Know that many women have had children successfully during medical school.

PLANNING

If you know, even before you start, that you might want to have a child during medical school, review your medical school options before committing to one. Grading policies, insurance, student health, support systems, childcare, geographic location, and overall curriculum can all impact your experience. While in school, your student affairs dean or other administrators can help you plan.

TIMING

While it's not always possible to plan, there are certain times during medical school that are more conducive to taking maternity leave. As the preclinical years are usually taught sequentially, it is not as easy to take a block of time off and rejoin; it may end up as a one-year leave of absence. Third-year clerkships and fourth year are more flexible in general (with the exception of residency application season). Your student affairs office may help you with schedule flexibility.

RESOURCES

Know what resources are out there to help you and be creative if you identify needs. There may be a parent support group at your school or you might join a babysitting co-op with other students or residents.

Childcare options

Having a solid plan is critical. Clinical rotations can have early hours, long days, and weekend duties. Weigh up all the options to find a situation that works for you.

+ Family: Often the most affordable, flexible, and reliable option, aid from family members may bring potential for relationship strain.

+ On-site hospital care: Can be reliable, affordable, and with extended hours to suit you, but there may be limited availability.

+ Daycare: Often affordable and reliable/trustworthy, but confined to more rigid hours.

+ Au-pair: Brings live-in childcare that can be flexible and reliable, but requires space and is limited to 45 hours a week.

+ Nanny/sitter: Offers flexible hours and convenience, but is often an expensive option that also has tax filing implications.

TIPS FOR MEDICAL STUDENT PARENTS

Being a medical student in a relationship is hard. Being a medical student and a parent is harder. Here are some tips to help you do it, because you can! Know that the skills you gain learning to balance the two worlds will help you throughout your career.

REDEFINE SUCCESS

You (or others around you) may have ideas of what a successful parent looks like—just throw those ideas out the window. You define success. Is your child safe? Are they developing and growing? Let go of the need to make homemade organic baby food. Accept your parenting "fails" with humor; you are doing your best and that is okay.

EFFICIENCY RULES

The more efficient you can be at work and home means more quality focused time with your family. Maybe that means incorporating clerkship studying during downtime in the team room, or prepping and freezing meals for the week ahead. Get class schedules as early as possible to help you plan your days.

CARE FOR YOURSELF

You will sometimes feel like you are being pulled in multiple directions, but you must make sure you have what you need to stay well. Use a jogging stroller to get in a run, or sneak in some mindful meditation.

OUTSOURCE WHEN YOU CAN

Have no guilt about outsourcing errands or tasks if it allows you more time to spend with your family. If you can afford it, invest in a cleaning service or meal prep service (or ask for this as a one-time or recurring gift).

ASK FOR HELP

Most importantly, ask for help if you need it! Put aside any pride and reframe it as trying to maximize your success as a student. If you are feeling overwhelmed, talk to a trusted advisor, find resources that can help, connect with peers, and/or confide in family. People all around you want to help you succeed, so let them.

SECURE ADEQUATE CHILDCARE

You will need time to study when you are not watching your children. Have a back-up plan for unexpected childcare needs. Family may be ideal but not always possible. See also Childcare Options, page 145.

"My kids were starting school when I was. The hardest thing was missing out on a lot of 'firsts.' What helped me was: #1 having a supportive spouse who was willing to record those memories, and #2 finding someone at school, whether fellow student or faculty, who could relate."

Maria Henry, PGY-3 in anesthesiology, University of Washington

"Being a parent and medical student will increase your organization and efficiency out of sheer survival needs."

PART

TOWARD
A CAREER

CHAPTER TWELVE

THRIVING ON CLINICAL CLERKSHIPS

Starting clinical rotations is a major milestone for a medical student. Now, you can finally apply your foundation of medical knowledge to actual patients and experience what it's like to be a member of the health care team.

You may likely feel both excited and nervous about the transition since it represents a seismic shift from how you have operated thus far. On clinical rotations, medical knowledge continues to be important, but now interpersonal communication and relationships, teamwork, clinical skills and reasoning, and work habits—the full integration of doctoring skills—take the stage.

Thriving on clinical clerkships means getting the most out of these formative experiences and engaging with your teams and patients in a meaningful way. It means incorporating feedback and becoming a better doctor. It means knowing your patients, advocating for them, and perhaps even feeling like you have made a difference in their lives. Some of these things are not captured by grades but will be significant in the development of your identity as a future physician.

Thriving on clinical clerkships also means maintaining your well-being while actively learning and growing as a medical student. As soon as you have your rotation schedule, plan out when you can fit in activities that will keep you healthy while bringing joy and much-needed breaks from long days in the clinic or hospital.

GETTING READY

You will be learning a lot by going on the wards, but it's also important to prepare well for the learning to come. You will need to get organized with resources and understand what will be expected of you generally, which will be refined with time. Clinical clerkships can be intense. Advanced thought and planning are needed to make sure you can reach all of your goals, both professional and personal.

"In your new role in a health care setting, you'll learn from, and contribute to, health care teams. Get to know your patients, read about them and each key topic, and make the most of everything you experience by being fully present. Be an advocate for your patients and make a difference!"

Dr. Terry Kind, Associate Dean for Clinical Education, George Washington University

BE PREPARED

Read up on any rotation orientation materials and talk to older peers to identify the important texts and resources you will use on the rotation. Peers who have gone through the rotation already will have valuable tips for you (particularly if they were at the same clinical sites). What are the general issues you will encounter on the rotation? What are the learning objectives of the rotation? Review before you start and take care of any onboarding logistics ahead of time.

MAKE SOME GOALS

Before each new rotation, set some goals. These may include general learning tasks as well as goals based on feedback from prior rotations. Make wellness goals for yourself, too—maybe plan to take a brief walk outside everyday, even during the workday, or to fit in a workout several days a week, or to continue seeing a therapist on a regular basis. Clinical rotations are busy, but your well-being is paramount for optimal learning and stress relief.

ANTICIPATE CHANGE

The rule of third year is that once you finally feel comfortable during one rotation, you switch to the next. Embrace change—it is temporary. Be both flexible and adaptable.

GET INTO THE RIGHT MINDSET

Keep in mind that your goal is to learn as much as you can from each rotation—this will make you a better doctor in whatever specialty you end up choosing. By seeking every opportunity to learn, and learning from each patient and all members of the health care team, you will get the most out of your education. Remember this may be the last time you have any involvement with this particular specialty—enjoy it and learn from it!

Top tips

EXCELLING ON CLERKSHIPS

To excel on clerkships, being a good team player and having a sincere attitude toward learning go a long way. Fourth-year medical student Garrett K. Berger shares his advice.

❶ Be present, always

Show up with the attitude of a team member and be present mentally and physically, even on a service you don't love. There is always something to learn.

❷ Take initiative

Don't wait to be told what to do. Instead, always look for ways to help the team within your role and do it.

❸ Follow through

If you tell your team you're going to do something, do it. You often hear about students saying "resident X told me to read up on indications for Y, but never asked me about it later!" Yes, residents are busy! Take a second and remind them.

❹ Be honest

If you mess up or forget to do something, admit it. If you don't know the answer to a question, that's okay. Look it up and follow through. And be honest about the specialty you're interested in on every rotation. I was honest about wanting to go into orthopedics from day one of M3 but made it clear that I was there to learn to be a physician first, surgeon second. On psychiatry, I got a patient with a fracture. On family medicine, I was assigned to the attending on sports medicine.

❺ Embrace it

You will likely work harder than you ever have before, but you'll also have a greater sense of purpose and reward. You're paying to be here. Make the best of it!

❻ Ask for help

If you're feeling down or overwhelmed, ask for help. Your course directors are there for this reason. So are you peers. Don't take it on alone.

ANATOMY OF A GOOD SOAP NOTE

The subjective, objective, assessment, and plan (SOAP) note is a standardized template for patient progress notes. On different clerkship rotations, there will be differences as to what is included and emphasized. Reviewing your intern's or resident's notes can be helpful, keeping in mind they may not always reflect best practices. The goal of all written notes is to clearly communicate and document a patient's condition and progress.

SUBJECTIVE

Streamlined and organized. Avoids judgmental or biased statements.

Relevant subjective information directly from the patient.

OBJECTIVE

Always starts with vitals, includes ranges and other objective measures if relevant.

Exam is **focused**, has adequate description. Includes patient's general appearance.

New lab results and studies since last report.

ASSESSMENT

Assessment **concisely** captures who patient is, working diagnosis, and current clinical status.

PLAN

Plan captures all planned work-up and treatment. With complex patients, combined A/P that has problem-based assessment and plans, listed in **priority order**, still with an overall global assessment.

Avoid making EMR pitfalls

+ When keeping electronic medical records (EMRs), don't copy and paste your assessment and plans forward, adding new information. Streamline and edit. Remove resolved items if no longer relevant.

+ If using a template, make sure that whatever is documented is something you personally have done/verified. Otherwise delete.

ORAL PRESENTATIONS

Oral presentations reflect your clinical skills, as well as your abilities to organize, report, and interpret data, which will help inform your clinical grade. Oral presentations should only represent a subset of information included on your written note and of the total information you know about any patient. Here is some advice on how to give excellent oral presentations.

ADAPT

Presentations will have specialty-specific differences, so be a great observer for cues when you first start a rotation. Different attendings may prefer certain things—find out their preferences. Some situations call for expedited presentations—always pay attention to environmental factors and respond accordingly.

BE CONCISE AND FOCUSED

Your goal is to give a clear, organized, focused presentation that provides just the right level of information. Focus on what's most relevant and important to discuss and skip the long-resolved issues. That means not presenting every lab value, but only what is relevant, including trends. Aim for a maximum of 3 minutes, 3–5 for new patient H&Ps (history and physical examination).

BE ORGANIZED

Follow the SOAP format for follow-up reports and the standard H&P format for new patients to stay organized and allow your listeners to follow along easily. Make sure you stick to what goes in each section—some students jump to interpretation and plan when they get to a physical exam finding or an abnormal lab value. Avoid editorial comments or asides when presenting. Stick to the format!

PREPARE

Have everything you need together in one place when about to present. You don't want to be shuffling papers around, looking for lab reports, and so on. Practice at home until your presentation flows—and it will eventually. Know that presenting well (especially if presenting with little notice and quickly organizing data and thoughts) is a skill that develops over time.

BE AN ORATOR

Speak clearly and loudly enough that no one has to strain to hear you. Aim for fluency, move from one section to the next without a long pause or waiting for approval. Present confidently—even if you feel unsure about some parts of your presentation. Make eye contact and avoid reading from your notes.

INCORPORATE FEEDBACK

Ask for specific feedback about your presentations from your residents and attendings and look for suggestions for making them even better. One clue to your presentation's effectiveness is to note what clarifying questions you are asked afterward, and what others need to add to give your attending the full story.

FEEDBACK: A CLINICAL STUDENT'S GOLD

Once you transition from the classroom to the clinical wards, it becomes harder to know how you are doing and how to improve. In an ideal world, you would receive regular feedback on your performance. However, the clinical environment can be busy, and supervisors, despite best intentions, may not initiate feedback sessions. Instead, be prepared to drive them yourself.

ASK TO MEET FOR FEEDBACK

Try to carve out time with your supervisor when both of you have time and can mentally prepare for the session. Remember that faculty want to help you succeed.

SELF-ASSESS

Consider your strengths and weaknesses. How are you progressing in the specific areas on which you are being evaluated (for example, history-taking, performing a physical examination, data synthesis)?

SET AND SHARE GOALS

Pinpoint areas for improvement and set measurable, attainable goals (see SMART thinking). Share these goals with your supervisor to help guide their feedback.

RECEIVE AND CLARIFY

Receive feedback with grace. It's critical to see constructive feedback as an opportunity to grow. Be sure to clarify any general feedback. If you hear, "Your presentations are good," ask what, specifically, is good about them and, importantly, ask how to take your presentations to the next level.

SMART thinking

The SMART goals framework produces clear, planned, and trackable objectives that are:

+ Specific

+ Measurable

+ Achievable

+ Relevant

+ Time-based

For example: I will include three differential diagnoses with each assessment and plan for the remainder of the clerkship.

"Don't focus on looking good—focus on being good. To be good, you have to consistently focus on getting better by seeking and incorporating feedback and constantly thinking about ways you can improve."

Paul Aronowitz, MD, Clerkship Director of Internal Medicine, University of California, Davis.

"Eliciting feedback (and acting on it) is an important skill to master in order to improve and be the best student (and future physician) you can be."

CLINICAL EVALUATIONS

During the preclinical years, most of your evaluations were likely based on medical knowledge assessment via exams. While you will continue to have exams on your clinical clerkships rotations, your performance will also be assessed via clinical evaluations that your supervising faculty (and sometimes residents) will complete. Areas assessed generally include the following categories:

COGNITIVE SKILLS

These include medical knowledge base, clinical reasoning and analytic skills, and organizational skills.

CLINICAL SKILLS

These involve data gathering, performing a physical examination, and technical and/or procedural skills.

INFORMATION PRESENTATION

Written notes and oral presentations, communication with patients and families, and patient education and counseling fall into this category.

INTERPERSONAL SKILLS

These include relationships with patients and families as well as those with professionals and colleagues.

PROFESSIONAL BEHAVIORS

Honest and ethical behavior, motivation for self-learning, an openness to feedback, an awareness of one's own limitations, and punctual, responsible, trustworthy behavior are all expected here.

Tips for OSCEs

During objective structured clinical examinations (OSCEs), you will demonstrate your clinical skills in a standardized scenario. They may occur as part of your clerkship grade or perhaps in between phases of medical school.

+ Be on your game: Arrive well-rested, on time, professionally dressed, neat in appearance, and with any necessary equipment.

+ Read instructions very carefully: You may only be doing one part of an encounter during any particular station. Know how much time you have.

+ Immerse yourself in the role: Yes, these are standardized patients, but try to imagine it is a real encounter and how you would handle the situation.

+ Remember the basics: Introduce yourself, wash your hands, confirm the patient's identity, ask open-ended questions, listen carefully, seek patient permission.

+ Be transparent: Verbalize your thoughts and actions as needed to be clear to the standardized patient/observer.

+ Relax! Try not to get too nervous. Remember that you know how to do this!

THE RIME FRAMEWORK

The RIME Framework, developed by Dr. Louis Pangaro, is one way to describe and monitor medical student progress on clinical rotations. Some schools use it as part of their clerkship evaluation process. Students generally progress through the stages in order, all requiring integration of knowledge, skills, and attitudes. Faculty may use the framework to give feedback to students. Students may use the framework to monitor their own progress and guide their individual learning goals.

Reporter — Accurately and reliably gathers and reports clinical information. Can focus data collection and presentation on central issues.

Interpreter — Identifies and prioritizes problems. Can develop a differential diagnosis independently with supporting evidence for and against each diagnosis.

Manager — Develops a diagnostic and therapeutic plan for each patient problem. Can analyze and tailor decisions based on an individual patient.

Educator — Educates patients and the team. Defines important questions to research and seeks to incorporate evidence-based medicine.

Pro tips

RIME FRAMEWORK PROGRESS

Early in their third year, students are generally expected to have good mastery of the reporter stage and to be actively working on development within the interpreter stage and early manager stage. By the end of the third year, students may have progressed to mastery of the interpreter stage and be working on developing their manager/educator skills.

CHAPTER THIRTEEN

CHOOSING A SPECIALTY

Some students come into medical school with well-formed plans to pursue a specific specialty, shaped by their prior experiences. Many do not. There can be a sense of pressure that you need to know what you want to specialize in early on, in order to start gaining specific experiences to help you match to residency. This is unnecessary pressure!

Choosing a specialty is a major life decision that will take time, career exploration, self-reflection, and many clinical experiences to confirm. It involves understanding the entire range of specialty options available, something few students are able to do prior to medical school. Many students who come into medical school believing they will pursue a specific residency eventually change their minds. This can and should be a thoughtful, non-rushed process in order to allow you to make the best decision for you.

Most students will want to make this decision by the end of the third year of medical school, but other students may need additional time into the following year. Some may even switch specialties while in residency. Whatever the timeline is for you, the final outcome should be a satisfying, rewarding career—the time and energy you spend getting there will ultimately be worth it.

This chapter covers the key principles and considerations involved in choosing a specialty, including first knowing yourself, career exploration options, specialty indecision, factoring in your competitiveness, parallel plans, and components of a residency application.

Look forward to discovering your future.

KNOW YOURSELF

The decision as to which specialty to pursue hinges upon knowing yourself. You are choosing a specialty that should match your interests, values, and skills. It is the specialty that will provide you with meaning and satisfaction through a long career, and fuel you forward when you are experiencing personal or professional challenges. That seems like a weighty, almost impossible task, but it really does start with knowing (or discovering) yourself and your interests in the context of medicine.

Self-assessments

There are many self-assessments out there that help students pinpoint their interests, values, and skills. For example, AAMC's Careers in Medicine website has many self-assessments that can help you know yourself in these key areas. Take these self-assessments early on in your medical school career to find potential specialties to explore. While your answers may change over time and with exposure to clinical situations, self-assessments can get you clued into the key questions and domains that you need to be considering. Take them again during the clinical years to see how things may have changed.

? INTERESTS

What subject matter is most fascinating to you? Do you like fast-paced environments or relish time to think through problems? Do you like to see a variety of things or the same thing but with a view to perfecting it? How much patient contact do you want? Are you looking for minimal or long-term relationships or somewhere in between? What patient populations do you enjoy interacting with the most? Do you crave breadth or depth of knowledge in your area of focus? Do you prefer immediate results or long-term outcomes?

? VALUES

How much will you value lifestyle in your future career—considerations such as work demands and leisure time? How much does the prestige of a specialty matter to you? How important is financial compensation? While all physicians make a comfortable living, some specialties, such as surgical subspecialties, make more. What will you find most meaningful in a future career in medicine?

? SKILLS

What skills do you want to use in your practice? Are you a pro at organizing people and coordinating logistics? Do you love working with your hands and want to do something procedural? Do you love talking and connecting with people? Do you love solving complicated problems?

"Don't forget about lifestyle of specialties. I knew that for me personally I love medicine, but I love things outside the hospital too. If you're happy spending 80 hours a week at the hospital, or doing overnight call often, that's great! If not, that's also great! Know yourself!"

Taylor Wahrenbrock, fourth-year medical student

SPECIALTIES BY COMPETITIVENESS

You can think of specialties in three tiers of competitiveness, related to supply and demand. While there is some fluidity year to year and it's more of a continuum than separate categories, this is a general way to think about the most common specialties.

Most competitive

Moderately competitive

Least competitive

Least competitive

+ Psychiatry**
+ Pediatrics
+ Physical medicine and rehabilitation
+ Neurology
+ Internal medicine
+ Pathology
+ Family medicine

Moderately competitive

+ Radiation oncology*
+ Obstetrics/gynecology
+ Anesthesiology
+ General surgery
+ Medicine pediatrics
+ Interventional radiology
+ Emergency medicine
+ Diagnostic radiology*

Most competitive

+ Plastic surgery
+ Neurosurgery
+ Otolaryngology
+ Cardiothoracic surgery
+ Vascular surgery
+ Orthopedic surgery
+ Ophthalmology
+ Dermatology
+ Urology

  * has decreased in competitiveness over recent years
 ** has increased in competitiveness over recent years

CAREER EXPLORATION

Specialty career exploration starts during your first year of medical school and continues through applying to residency (and sometimes beyond that).

PRECLINICAL

The preclinical years are the time to learn about all specialties. Many resources exist online, at your school, and through books and podcasts. Know the full scope of specialties, including lesser-known ones and combined residencies.

"**Don't discount negative experiences; reflect on them and figure out what attitudes, actions, and activities made them negative. Assess subsequent experiences accordingly. I cannot overemphasize the role of reflection.**"

Tomi Ifelayo, fourth-year medical student

→ TAKE SELF-ASSESSMENTS
As mentioned previously, self-assessments help you to get to know yourself and point to areas for further exploration. Some are backed by a lot of data.

→ OBSERVE AND REFLECT AFTER CLINICAL EXPOSURE
You may have an early clinical exposure program at your school or be able to volunteer at a free clinic or similar. Reflect about what you enjoy and do not particularly enjoy about these clinical experiences. What components of these do you want in your future career?

→ JOIN SPECIALTY INTEREST GROUPS
These student-run groups can expose you to physicians in the field and specialty-related content. You could even assume a leadership role over time.

→ SHADOW PHYSICIANS
Through either formal shadowing programs offered through your school or informally through your own reach outs, you can get a glimpse of a day in the life.

→ DO CLINICAL RESEARCH
Clinical research in a specialty can help you learn more about the specialty and work with a faculty mentor in that field.

→ JOIN PROFESSIONAL SOCIETIES
You can join as a student member and potentially also attend conferences (or participate on student committees) to get to know a specialty of interest.

CLINICAL

Once you start to gain hands-on experience via clinical rotations, you will gain valuable information with each clerkship about what you like and don't like.

"**Explore opportunities to learn about specialties even outside of traditional rotations. Ask everyone you work with 'why this specialty?' And it always helps if you have a close friend who can give you another view of when you seemed happiest.**"

Harleen Marwah, fourth-year medical student

→ SEEK ENRICHING EXPERIENCES

Following a patient on medicine who needs a procedure by another service and would love to see it? Ask your team. The worst they can do is say no. You could get interesting exposure to different specialties or subspecialties, as well as be there with your patient.

→ TALK TO EVERYONE ABOUT THEIR SPECIALTY

Clerkship faculty and directors, residents, and older peers on your service can give you insights into how and why they chose their specialty and how content they are with that decision. Keep in mind that there are always disgruntled people in every specialty so seek a variety of people and views. Also seek out people in different settings (community versus university hospital) and practices for a more complete understanding.

→ BE INTENTIONAL WITH EACH CLERKSHIP

Ruling out a specialty is progress, but also stop to think why it is not for you. You might find it helpful to keep a journal to write down salient experiences within each clerkship—patients, interactions, meaningful moments. The third year goes by quickly; keeping track of your thoughts and feelings can come in very handy later.

→ KEEP YOUR EYES OPEN

You won't be able to formally rotate in all specialties during third year, but you can seek exposure to other specialties during each clerkship. You can be in the emergency room while admitting patients in other core clerkship specialties, go down to radiology to read films with the radiologists, and visit pathology to look at peripheral smears or joint aspirations. You can notice what the anesthesiologists do in the operating room and the work that consulting services do.

→ ENGAGE IN SCHOLARSHIP

Beyond doing clinical research, you can also write up clinical vignettes or case reports in the specialty, hopefully resulting in future presentations or even publications. You could find a faculty mentor this way.

SPECIALTY INDECISION

You have narrowed it down to two or more specialties. How to make that final decision? Here are some strategies.

TALK TO MORE PEOPLE

Find faculty and residents in each specialty and learn more about what they like most and do not like most about their work. Find people who can give you an honest appraisal. Older attendings can share what they have grown weary of over the years. Talk to a career advisor (faculty or dean) about your indecision to help you process it.

WRITE PERSONAL STATEMENTS

Write separate personal statements for each specialty and see which one is most compelling. One might feel truer to your authentic self. Have a friend read these and give you input.

TRY ON A SPECIALTY

Pretend that you have made the decision for one specialty and "try on" what that feels like for a week or two. Then switch specialties for the next week or two. You may notice a difference in how you feel.

TAKE A SELF-ASSESSMENT

There are self-assessments specifically for specialty indecision to help you pinpoint why you are having trouble making the decision and what information you may need to seek. See the AAMC Careers in Medicine site for one.

TAKE ADVANCED ELECTIVES

Doing advanced, fourth-year-level electives can help you make that final decision as you will see what it is like to work in the specialty with a higher level of responsibility. Some students find it helpful to take electives in the separate specialties back-to-back for contrast.

SELF-REFLECT

Revisit the "Know Yourself" page and dig deep into your personal values, interests, and skills and how they relate to the specialties in question. Lean heavily on your clerkship experiences and gut feelings. Will what you find exciting about a specialty now still be exciting when you are 40 or 50 years old?

TAKE MORE TIME

Sometimes, you just need more time. Consider dual-applying and continuing to process and reflect during applications and interview season. Often, students settle on an answer by the time rank lists are due, or may rank both specialties and feel that they could be happy in either.

> "You must be able to handle the 'worst' aspects of any specialty and embrace the 'bread and butter' issues and situations."

FACTORING IN YOUR COMPETITIVENESS

Being realistic about your chances of matching into your desired specialty is key. If odds are slim, you might consider a different specialty or you should at least be prepared with a back-up (or "parallel") plan that you are comfortable with. But how do you gauge your competitiveness and what to do with that information?

Do what you love

Keep in mind that you have options within the different tiers of specialty competitiveness to do what you find most fulfilling. Discuss options with a career advisor.

For example:

+ Love procedures but not competitive enough for a surgical specialty? Consider subspecialty internal medicine or pediatrics like gastrointestinal, cardiology, and critical care.

+ Love women's health but not competitive enough for obstetrics/gynecology? You can practice full-spectrum family medicine and deliver babies or practice women's health in internal medicine.

LOOK AT EXISTING MATCH DATA

Numerous resources exist with data on applicants who match to particular specialties. The National Resident Matching Program (NRMP) releases both applicant match data and program director survey data on the most important factors for interview selection and matching. There are also student-reported national datasets available, and many schools have internal match data for prior graduates. Discuss this data with your career advisor or mentor for best context.

DISCUSS WITH FACULTY AND ADVISORS

Meet with faculty in the specialty to go over your individual application components (see pages 170–171) for their assessment of your competitiveness. Your student affairs dean can also provide important insights on how students from your institutions have done and how to maximize your chances of success.

GAUGE YOUR COMMITMENT

Getting into an über-competitive specialty may take more than one application cycle, a research year off, or moving your research pursuits into overdrive. Are you willing to invest this time and energy? If not, consider an alternative specialty that you would be happy doing that is less competitive.

PARALLEL PLANS

Every student applying to a highly competitive specialty or a student who is at risk for not matching into their desired specialty should have a solid back-up plan that has been thoughtfully constructed ahead of application season. This is insurance that you hopefully won't need to use, but if something happens, you'll be thankful to have it.

DUAL-APPLY TO A LESS COMPETITIVE SPECIALTY

If there's another specialty that you feel you could be happy in, consider dual-applying. This adds a layer of complexity to your residency application season but could be an important back-up plan.

TAKE A RESEARCH YEAR

If the reason you might not match is because of lack of research, consider taking a year to do dedicated research and reapply with the next cycle or the cycle after that.

DO A PRELIMINARY INTERN YEAR

Sometimes, doing a preliminary year in surgery or medicine can help bolster an application where there might be clinical weaknesses. Keep in mind that intern year is very busy though, and you would be applying and interviewing during that time. Some students continue on in a categorical program in the same institution since they are now known and have a good record.

GET ANOTHER DEGREE

Some students might opt to obtain another degree—MPH, MS, MBA, and so on—and then reapply if it aligns with their overall career goals.

Dual-applying tips

1. Write separate personal statements and clearly label them as such, so there is no confusion when assigning them to the different programs.

2. Consider having separate letter writers for the two different applications. If they overlap, ensure that the letter writer is aware that you are dual-applying and make the letters agnostic of specialty or have two separate letters.

3. Be prepared for a question on interviews, such as "Are you also applying to X specialty?"

4. Attempt to do research that could fit with both specialties.

5. Limit applying to different specialties at the same institutions. Note that this would not normally come to anyone's attention but it will avoid stress and potential conflict.

6. Talk to a trusted advisor about your application and thoughts throughout the process; discuss your uncertainties and strategy.

COMPONENTS OF A
RESIDENCY APPLICATION

Your residency application will present who you are as an applicant to programs and will include objective grades and performance during medical school, your activities, research, leadership, and accomplishments, as well as a glimpse into you personally—through a personal statement you write and letters of recommendation from faculty you worked with. As you put this together, think about the key qualities and experiences that make you unique and that you want program directors to know about you. Then, make sure this comes through in your application.

PERSONAL INFORMATION

Your basic contact and demographic information.

CURRICULUM VITAE

This is like a resume, but is more comprehensive. It tells your full professional story in terms of education, work experience, extracurricular activity involvement, scholarly activity, research, skills, honors, awards, certifications, and hobbies. Seek guidance and feedback when constructing to ensure it is organized and clear, and includes the right level of detail.

PERSONAL STATEMENT

Gives reviewers an idea of who you are as a person and why you are interested in your specialty. A great personal statement allows reviewers a window into you, your unique qualities and perspective, and leaves them wanting to meet you in person.

LETTERS OF RECOMMENDATION

These letters are written by faculty members you have worked with (mainly in a clinical capacity) and speak to your strengths as an applicant. It can help when you ask potential writers whether they feel

Pro tips

BE HONEST

In your application and residency interviews, present who you are, not who you think program directors want you to be. Programs seek different types of applicants. By being authentic and true to your personality and interests, you will be more likely to end up at a program that is an excellent fit and somewhere you will thrive.

When you don't want to do a residency

Maybe doing a residency has little appeal for you and you would like to pursue an alternative career path.

This might include:

+ Policy
+ Public health
+ Consulting
+ Biotechnology
+ Journalism/writing
+ Bench/laboratory research
+ Other

Talk to your advisor or student affairs dean about your interests, as well as others who have chosen an alternative path. Sometimes doing a residency first can help you reach future goals and sometimes it makes sense to skip residency. Regardless, it's important to think through this step as applying to residency later on can be challenging.

they can write you a strong letter—this gives them (and you) an out if they think someone else might be able to write a stronger letter on your behalf.

TRANSCRIPT
Your medical school transcript with all of the courses and grades you have received so far. You will also have a transcript of your board scores.

MEDICAL STUDENT PERFORMANCE EVALUATION
Aka "The Dean's Letter," this is a letter prepared by your school that follows a standard template and describes your academic performance throughout medical school. Typically, this includes how you did on each core clerkship rotation and places your performance in context with that of your peers.

"Some of my classmates chose a specialty in high school and some decided during sophomore year of college. Some decided in October of third year, others two months before submitting residency applications. Everyone's journey is different."

Reem Al Shabeeb, fourth-year medical student

PART

CHAPTER FOURTEEN

PROFESSIONAL IDENTITY

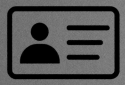

Every student goes through a transformation during medical school—from lay person upon acceptance to young physician upon graduation. During these formative times, you will integrate the knowledge, skills, values, and behaviors of a competent, ethical, humanistic physician with your own identity.

It is the goal of your medical school to provide the education, experiences, and socialization to facilitate your growth into the physician you are meant to become. Your part is not passive; you will be called upon to engage, to reflect, to be self-aware, and to continually strive to learn, to grow, and to improve. You may be faced with times that test your professionalism and ethics and will need to navigate these situations to make decisions that align with your values.

This chapter touches upon some areas involved in the development of your professional identity and the overlapping concept of professionalism, including school honor codes, combating threats to your professionalism, and engaging in social justice and advocacy.

Notably, your professional identity is not static and will continue to grow and develop over time as a practicing physician. In addition, while some tenets of medical professionalism are core to the profession, such as the primacy of patient welfare, professionalism is also a sociocultural concept that can evolve over time.

You will have many times during medical school when you do something and think, "Wow, I feel like an actual doctor!" Bask in this feeling and the honor that comes with it as you move closer to your future you.

WHITE COAT CEREMONY

The White Coat Ceremony is an event that marks an important milestone in your journey toward becoming a physician. Often occurring in the first days of medical school, this is when you have your white coat placed on your shoulders and symbolically take on the values and professional responsibility of the medical profession you are entering and acknowledge your central obligation of caring for patients.

REFLECT ON THE SIGNIFICANCE The white coat represents the aspirational values of medicine: humility, compassion, integrity, accountability, ethics, and humanism. Reflect on this significance in advance of the ceremony. During the ceremony, be aware of how you feel. Revisit this moment later on whenever you need a reminder of why you are doing this and what it all means.

COMMEMORATE THE DAY Families are often invited to the White Coat Ceremony. Whether or not they can attend, share the day and moment with them. Remember to thank those who supported you to get here.

TYPICAL COMPONENTS While schools may differ in what they include in the ceremony, it typically includes recitation of an oath, speakers, and presentation of the white coat or other symbol (for example, a stethoscope).

BE PHOTO READY Photographs will document this milestone—dress professionally and avoid anything bulky that would make putting on the white coat challenging.

HOLD YOUR OWN SPECIAL EVENT
If your school does not have a White Coat Ceremony, create your own special event with family and friends to honor your entry into the profession.

"I still remember exactly how I felt when I put on the white coat for the first time during our White Coat Ceremony, and I go back to that feeling a lot when I'm tired or burned out in residency. It reminds me of why I chose medicine in the first place."

Michelle Chen, PGY-3 in anesthesiology

HONOR CODES

When you enter medical school, you most likely will be required to abide by an honor code that governs professional and ethical student behavior, in concert with your school's professionalism policy. Elements of school honor codes generally include the following areas.

ACADEMIC HONESTY

+ Having integrity in one's work
+ No cheating (giving or receiving aid), plagiarism, or falsifying/manipulating information/data for one's own gain
+ Conducting research truthfully; giving due credit to work done by others
+ Accurately reporting all patient-related findings, test results, and other data

RESPECT FOR OTHERS

+ Treating patients, peers, faculty, and staff with respect, the essence of humanism
+ Contributing to a classroom atmosphere conducive to learning
+ Maintaining patient confidentiality
+ Resolving conflicts with peers in a way that respects the dignity of all
+ Recognizing and speaking out against discrimination and bias

COMMITMENT TO EXCELLENCE

+ Striving for excellence in the pursuit of knowledge and development of skills
+ Recognizing one's limits and seeking assistance if needed
+ Avoiding substance use that could interfere with clinical responsibilities
+ Conducting oneself professionally in all medical settings

Advisors can help students learn from professionalism lapses.

Infractions

Violation of the honor code may result in disciplinary action. Infractions are often handled by an honor council or board, which can include peers and/or the dean.

Violations may be categorized into severity levels, with sanctions given accordingly. Importantly, serious or repeated infractions may result in a formal notation in the student's Dean's Letter that is submitted as part of residency applications, and this can place students at risk for not matching to a residency program. Infractions may even result in dismissal from medical school.

Students in distress may be more tempted to compromise their professional and ethical standards; seek help before this happens.

ALTRUISM

+ Putting patients' interests first
+ Setting patient care as the highest priority in the clinical setting

ACCOUNTABILITY

+ Being accountable for one's own behavior and actions
+ Holding peers accountable for violations of the honor code

NURTURING YOUR INNER PHYSICIAN

Your inner physician starts to develop even before medical school and goes into a transformational growth phase during medical school. How do you nurture this growth?

PRACTICE MINDFULNESS
Mindfulness and self-awareness are essential for professional identity formation.

ENGAGE IN THE HUMANITIES
Art, literature, and history help foster reflection and broaden perspectives. Many medical schools offer cultural experiences aimed at cultivating deeper understanding and awareness.

BE A PHYSICIAN CITIZEN
Rather than silo off from the world around you during medical school, remain aware of what is going on and your place in society as an individual and future physician.

VALUE RELATIONSHIPS
Professional, meaningful relationships with peers, faculty mentors, and patients will spur and foster your development.

CULTIVATE RESILIENCE AND WELL-BEING
Cultivating habits of mind and practices that build your resilience and well-being will allow your inner physician to thrive.

The hidden curriculum

The hidden curriculum refers to practices taught outside of formal teaching, which conflict with the professional values you have committed to as a future physician. You may see residents acting in ways that oppose those values, perhaps due to cynicism or burnout. Here are ways to address such eventualities.

+ **Identify**: Once the hidden curriculum is identified, it's no longer "hidden" and can be addressed. Instead of enduring it, identify it so your professional identity can thrive despite it.

+ **Discuss**: When you receive conflicting messages, reflect on them and discuss with peers, or a trusted faculty advisor. How to reconcile these messages?

+ **Write**: Writing about these conflicts can be a powerful way to process them.

+ **Challenge**: Challenging bias takes courage, particularly as a student, but if done with respect and humility, it may effect change.

+ **Aspire**: Find those role models who embody professionalism in everything they do. Gain inspiration from their example.

SOCIAL JUSTICE AND ADVOCACY

Three fundamental principles of medical professionalism are the primacy of patient welfare; the principle of patient autonomy; and the principle of social justice. This last principle calls on us to promote justice in the health care system and to address health care disparities. As a medical student, you may feel called to join efforts to raise awareness and advocate for social justice.

DEVELOP KNOWLEDGE AND SKILLS

Arm yourself with the necessary knowledge and skills to understand current health care injustices and the skills needed to effectively advocate. Some medical schools have this built into their curriculum and, at others, you may need to seek this information through extracurricular pursuits.

USE YOUR VOICE

As a physician-to-be, you have a voice in the public sphere. Consider sharing evidence-based information and advocating through writing opinion editorials, social media posts, and/or even assisting with local or national legislative efforts to address health care disparities.

JOIN ADVOCACY GROUPS

This could be student interest groups and/or national health care advocacy groups. These communities of like-minded peers can be sources of support and meaning.

PARTICIPATE IN RESEARCH ON HEALTH CARE DISPARITIES

You can engage in research that is aimed at understanding or addressing health care disparities and connect with faculty who are passionate about the same things you are.

FIND FACULTY MENTORS

Identifying and aligning with faculty mentors engaged in this work can be motivating and inspiring, as well as provide needed support.

KNOW RELEVANT SCHOOL POLICIES

Learn about relevant policies and the potential positive and negative impacts of engaging in different kinds of advocacy.

Pro tips

ACT PROFESSIONALLY

Freedom of speech does not mean freedom from social or professional consequences. It's important to fully appreciate how using your voice can result in meaningful change and influence public opinion, but can also lead to increased public scrutiny. Be sure your advocacy is lawful and reflects your professional values.

SOCIAL MEDIA

Social media offers powerful communication tools that keep us connected and engaged with the world around us. It is critically important for you to consider your social media presence and whether it reflects your value system as a future physician. Throughout your career (regardless of whether in medicine), your social media presence and digital footprint may be used to assess your character, fitness, and job candidacy. Medical students have been dismissed from medical school for inappropriate social media posts and doctors have been fired or have received sanctions from their state boards for inappropriate online behavior.

THINK BEFORE YOU POST

Anything you post online becomes part of your digital footprint and nothing can be truly deleted from digital memory. A momentary lapse in judgment can be captured by screenshot and live on, even from a "private" account. Use the "Grandma test": would you be comfortable if your grandmother (or dean) saw your post?

BE RESPECTFUL

Be respectful in your interactions with others online.

CONSIDER YOUR CONNECTIONS

Who are you comfortable being connected to on your social media accounts? Being connected to patients on a personal account may be at best awkward and, at worst, an ethical issue.

REFLECT AND ASSESS

As you enter medical school and the medical profession, reflect on your social media presence—is there anything that no longer reflects who you are now? Consider removing or archiving those posts.

AVOID POSTING PATIENT INFORMATION

Safeguarding patient privacy and abiding by the Health Insurance Portability and Accountability Act of 1996 (HIPAA) is paramount. Posting specific patient information is never essential and can put you at risk for inadvertently violating HIPAA law.

TRACK YOUR DIGITAL FOOTPRINT

Periodically, do an internet search of your name to see what shows up about you. This is what potential employers and patients may see. If there is inaccurate or damaging information, you can try to take steps to remove it.

LEVERAGE FOR PROFESSIONAL GROWTH

Once you are comfortable and secure with your use and have reflected on your digital identity (see opposite), you may choose to use social media to learn, advocate, and innovate. Identify role models who do this well and learn from them.

KNOW YOUR INSTITUTIONS' SOCIAL MEDIA POLICIES

Your medical school and affiliated clinical sites may have their own social media policies. Be sure you understand and adhere to their guidance.

SOCIAL MEDIA IN MEDICINE'S HIERARCHY OF NEEDS

Chretien and Kind described a Social Media in Medicine's Hierarchy of Needs for social media use in medicine, which is a pyramid of needs sitting on a foundation of public trust. The lowest, most basic needs must be met before reaching higher levels. While not everyone will want to aspire to the highest level, "discovery," the first two levels are essential to modern practice and social media use.

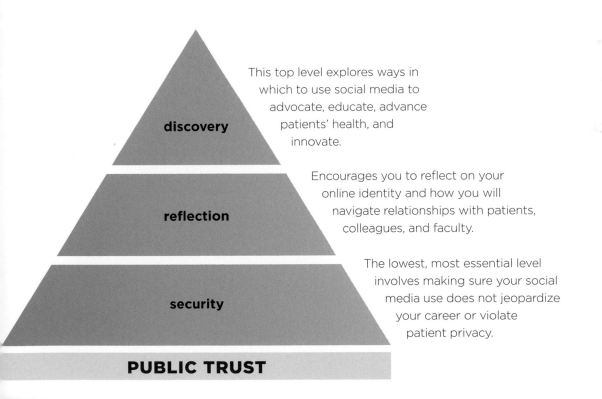

discovery

This top level explores ways in which to use social media to advocate, educate, advance patients' health, and innovate.

reflection

Encourages you to reflect on your online identity and how you will navigate relationships with patients, colleagues, and faculty.

security

The lowest, most essential level involves making sure your social media use does not jeopardize your career or violate patient privacy.

PUBLIC TRUST

CHAPTER FIFTEEN

DIVERSITY, EQUITY, AND INCLUSION

Medical schools seek a diverse student body in all forms—race, socioeconomic status, rural versus urban, life experiences, gender and sexual orientation, age, and more—in order to produce future physicians who will best care for the full spectrum of patients. You and your unique interests and lived experiences bring an important perspective to your medical school class.

Diversity within a medical school class and within the medical profession at large is critical. But having diversity alone is not enough. Equity is about ensuring that everyone has access to the same opportunities, despite some enjoying advantages and some facing barriers—not everyone starts from the same place. And inclusion is about diverse identities feeling valued, welcomed, and included.

We all play a role in creating an inclusive learning environment that values the unique contributions of all members. This includes recognizing and reducing the effect of our own implicit biases, responding to microaggressions and discrimination of ourselves or our peers, and standing up to injustices. This chapter delves into these topics, as well as discussing how to embrace your diversity and being a woman in medicine. It is for every reader of this book.

Allow yourself to be enriched by learning in the presence of diverse peers, faculty, and patients during medical school. And embrace your own diversity and the unique contributions you will make to medicine.

IMPLICIT BIAS

We all carry implicit bias—that is, bias that we unconsciously carry with us as we interact with others. While you may commit to treating all patients (and colleagues) equally and fully intend this, be aware that your implicit bias can, and does, have influence over your actions.

Race/ethnicity implicit bias is common, as is that of other characteristics, such as gender, socioeconomic status, age, substance use, and disability. The following strategies can help you reduce the effect implicit bias has on your treatment of others.

AWARENESS AND ACKNOWLEDGMENT

Take the Implicit Association Test to uncover your own implicit biases. Understand that the instinct to categorize and stereotype is a normal aspect of human cognitive processes, and that acknowledging them can help you address them.

INDIVIDUATION

See a person as an individual. Learn about their unique history and context. When you become aware that your response is based on stereotype, consciously acknowledge and adjust.

GREATER EMPATHY

Imagining yourself in a person's shoes helps counter activation of stereotypes. Similarly, greater empathy levels are associated with less stereotypic attitudes.

A WIDER SOCIAL SPHERE

Seek to interact with people of different backgrounds and identities than you and approach with cultural humility.

PARTNERSHIP BUILDING

With patients, consider your relationship as one of collaboration versus that of one involving high status (provider) and low status (patient).

EMOTIONAL REGULATION

Your own stress and negative emotions can lead to a greater tendency to stereotype and deploy unconscious prejudices. Attend to your own emotional well-being and stay vigilant of any potential bias when you are feeling stressed.

The Implicit Association Test

This freely available tool measures the strength of associations between concepts (for example, Black people, older people) and evaluations (good, bad) or stereotypes. Having implicit biases does not mean you are prejudiced and may be the opposite of what you consciously believe. Those of stigmatized groups may show a preference for the majority group. Acknowledge these automatic thoughts and you can work on reducing their influence.

"Implicit bias in health care professionals contributes to health care disparities and poorer quality of care."

MICROAGGRESSIONS

Microaggressions are brief and common indignities toward marginalized individuals and groups that cumulatively generate as much or more stress than overt discrimination. Understanding why something can be perceived as a microaggression, its effects on the recipients, and how to respond when experienced or witnessed can contribute to an improved learning and work environment for all. In contrast, discrimination involves the unfair treatment of individuals based on race, gender, religion, disability, sexual orientation, age, social class, and more, and exists at the level of the individual or the system (for example, policies).

"Physicians, as leaders, must have the words and communication skills to interact, interpret, and navigate uncomfortable and distressing situations where they feel disrespected or discriminated against by their patients or health care teams in the clinical setting."

Susan Cheng, Ed.L.D., MPP, Senior Associate Dean for Diversity, Equity, & Inclusion and creator of the Stop, Talk, Roll framework, Georgetown University School of Medicine

Subtypes of microaggressions

Microassault:
This is often intentional, blatant, and intended to offend the recipient. The focus is on the individual versus the group: "You people are all the same"; "Are they letting women be doctors now?"

Microinsult:
A subtle snub that is demeaning and communicates insensitivity to a person's identity. It is often unconscious—for example, when providers are confused with the nurse or hospital support staff. Other examples include pathologizing a person's behavior or communication style: "You speak English well."

Microinvalidation:
Often unconscious, this excludes or negates the personal thoughts, feelings, or experiential reality of a person. It supports the myth of meritocracy (that race, sex, socioeconomic status, and so on, do not impact achievement).

"You people are all the same"

"You speak English well."

COPING WITH MICROAGGRESSIONS

Christian Hendrix, an internal medicine resident at St. Louis University, shares her advice and lessons learned on coping with microaggressions as a Black female medical student, while realizing the impact racism has on medicine.

❶ It's them, not you
Sometimes, when you've observed that you are being treated differently, it may be a good idea to initially question what actions you can do differently. But always remember that more times than not, it could be a personal issue on their end.

❷ Don't take on the burden of combating stereotypes
It is not your job to combat stigma or stereotypes. For instance, if I am the only Black female within an academic setting, and I speak up to answer a question and am incorrect, I have to remember that this does not reflect the knowledge of all Black females. And if others affirm negative stereotypes about Black females because of my actions, that's on them, not me.

❸ Tactfully respond to microaggressions
Find the courage to respond to microaggressions or discriminatory words that are aimed at either yourself or a colleague. The most helpful ways that work for me include practicing responses, which can be as simple as "Ouch," or "Hmmm, don't know about that." In addition, you can provide education on why certain words or actions are inappropriate.

❹ Seek and give support to your peers
Remember friends and colleagues who may share similar experiences. They may provide solace for your exhaustion. They can also likely share perspective on specific instances. Their support is invaluable.

❺ Reach out to your diversity office
The diversity office often drives innovation and change within an institution. It also likely has important relationships with key stakeholders and can communicate concerns with others on a personal level or over a wide network.

RESPONDING TO MICROAGGRESSIONS AND DISCRIMINATION

How do you handle microaggressions from patients or health care team members? Follow these steps and suggestions for what to say in these situations.

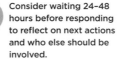

Follow the appropriate steps, depending on who you are dealing with.

 Reach out to deans, faculty, or peers for immediate support.

Consider waiting 24-48 hours before responding to reflect on next actions and who else should be involved.

STOP

Keep appropriate distance in case of escalation.

TALK

Talk through the situation with your supervising resident or physician.

Stop communication. Immediately consult with attending.

Assess patient for source of hostility

- Angry/frustrated patient?

- Intoxicated with substances?

- Psychiatric/delirium/dementia or other medical conditions?

"I am not comfortable with your comments. I am going to consult with the supervising physician to ensure you receive the appropriate care."

"I want the best care for you so I'm going to get the supervising physician so we can discuss together."

"I'd like to process what just happened on my rotation and get your advice and support."

"Dr. M, the other day when you mentioned '....,' I felt uncomfortable because this could have been offensive to [group of people]."

"I'm not sure what happened but I need to talk through something with you."

Consider having a private conversation with the individual. Stay calm, with an even tone, and allow the person to react and give their side.

ROLL

Observe and learn how a superior handles the situation.

Roll out and get support.

Judge the situation moving forward.

"Could we debrief the patient situation that just happened?"

Resolved: Continue on.

"Can you talk me through how to handle this situation?"

Unresolved: Seek help via your Office for Diversity and Inclusion, faculty, or student affairs dean.

BEING AN ALLY

If you have the privilege and power of being in a majority group, you can work on being an ally for those who are not. Keep in mind that you earn the label of "ally" through your consistent actions to understand and support others; it is not a designation that you give yourself.

ACKNOWLEDGE YOUR PRIVILEGE

Acknowledge that you have privilege and that others bear a burden that is hard for you to fully understand.

EDUCATE YOURSELF

Take the time and energy to understand the historical underpinnings of racism and discrimination. Seek to understand the perspectives of your peers who belong to minority groups.

ADVOCATE

Join local or national advocacy efforts that work toward systemic change to combat oppression and health care disparities. Support causes that champion equal rights, justice, respect, and dignity for all.

SUPPORT

Support your peers, staff, and faculty who experience mistreatment.

DOCUMENT AND REPORT

Use your school's reporting mechanisms to document and report what you perceive to be mistreatment based on identity status.

CHALLENGE

Use your privilege and voice to challenge policies or practices that create barriers for specific people and groups.

Be an upstander

An upstander is the opposite of a bystander. Be empowered to challenge statements or actions that make you uncomfortable and appear to reflect bias or harassment based on identity. Focus on the behaviors you witness, not the person, and use a calm, nonconfrontational approach to give the person a chance to apologize, reflect, and learn.

1. **Notice that something is happening**

2. **Decide that it needs to be addressed**

3. **Say something:**

   Ask neutral questions to clarify a person's intentions. This can promote dialogue and reflection.

   Be direct and honest: Stating that you are uncomfortable with a situation can provide a moment for others to react as well.

   Use humor: Sometimes humor can diffuse a situation.

4. **In private, offer support to affected individuals**

MISTREATMENT

Medical student mistreatment can happen to any student, and occurs at higher rates to gender, racial, and sexual orientation minorities. Recurrent mistreatment can lead to burnout and ranges from public humiliation to gender and racial discrimination. Yet, student mistreatment often goes unreported because students do not believe anything will result from their report or they fear retribution.

Examples of mistreatment

+ Belittlement or humiliation

+ Discrimination on the basis of race, gender, sexual orientation, gender identity, religion, ethnic background, age, or physical ability or appearance

+ Disregard for the safety of others

+ Insults or verbal attacks

+ Sexual harassment

+ Taking credit for another individual's work

+ Threatening to assign a lower grade or to write a poor evaluation as a means of intimidation

KNOW YOUR SCHOOL'S MISTREATMENT POLICY

All schools have a policy on mistreatment—be familiar with this from the beginning of medical school. Mistreatment can happen at any time and by professors, staff, patients, residents, and attendings.

WRITE IT DOWN

If you believe you have been subject to mistreatment, write it down. When it happened, who else was present, and where you were.

CONFIDE IN SOMEONE YOU TRUST

Sometimes, you need to process and talk through what happened. Find someone you trust—a faculty advisor, dean, or peer—to have a confidential conversation.

REPORT MISTREATMENT

Schools will not know what is happening unless incidents are reported. Follow your school's procedures for reporting. There may be an ombudsman for student mistreatment—a neutral mediator—who can help you process and tell you what steps to take next.

GET SUPPORT

Look to peers, mentors, advisors, family, and/or a therapist for support.

EMBRACING YOUR DIVERSITY

You were chosen to be a medical student based on your unique identities and path to medical school. During medical school, there's sometimes pressure to hide or "cover" those identities, to the detriment of one's sense of self. Remember that your goal is to hold on to your authentic self. This is part of the richness you bring to medicine and the world.

REFLECT ON YOUR UNIQUENESS

What identities make you, you? What aspects of yourself do you want to safeguard during medical school?

CONNECT WITH IDENTITY GROUPS

Find and join the student organizations that honor your identity and allow you to find support in fellow students and faculty advisors.

FIND SUPPORTIVE MENTORS AND ROLE MODELS

Remember that mentors can be peer mentors who are a little ahead of you in school or faculty, staff, or deans. Mentors can help support your personal and professional growth. Mentors may share your identity or belong to other identity groups but fully embrace diversity and inclusion. See Chapter Eight: Finding a Mentor and Being a Mentee.

KEEP YOUR INNER CIRCLE CLOSE

In Chapter Eleven, we talked about the support your inner circle of your closest family and friends provides. These are your champions and will help keep you grounded in your identity.

SEEK TO LEARN FROM OTHERS DIFFERENT THAN YOU

In medicine, we can all learn from one another, and curiosity and learning about others different than us can help us care for all patients with true empathy.

"Your family will always be there to support you. And they want you to have true happiness, with or without medical school. By sharing the details of your path to and through medical school with them, they will offer some of the best support money cannot buy."

Christian Hendrix, PGY-1 in internal medicine

WOMEN IN MEDICINE

There are more women entering medical school than ever, with women now outnumbering men. However, there still exist challenges for women in medicine. Women are not as well represented in higher academic ranks and continue to experience gender and sexual harassment and discrimination. Here are ways to thrive as a woman in medical school.

FIND WOMEN ROLE MODELS

Role models in medicine can show you a path to the future you envision, whether that is achieving balance in having a career and having a family or thriving as a woman in a male-dominated specialty.

SUPPORT OTHER WOMEN

Step in (if safe) when you see harassment occurring. If a woman's idea is ignored in a small group but then embraced when a man says it, amplify her voice. "That is what Emma said, and I agree."

CORRECT GENDER BIASES

When you are mistaken for the nurse or social worker by a patient, simply correct them. "I'm actually the student doctor who will be caring for you."

BE YOU, BE PROUD

You may feel a pull to be someone you are not—that you need to act in certain ways to be more accepted. Some women feel the need to take on more masculine qualities to show leadership or more feminine qualities to avoid being negatively labeled. Accept and reconnect with who you are. Women bring necessary diversity to medicine that results in better patient care and better health care institutions. Own your personal style and be proud.

TAKE CARE OF YOURSELF

Invest in your well-being and safeguard it. Practice mindfulness, cultivate your resilience, and make sure you have guardrails to keep you on track. Some women have difficulty saying no and wind up overcommitted and derive less satisfaction from their engagements. Remember that saying no sometimes is saying yes to yourself.

SEEK HELP IF YOU ARE HARASSED

Report harassment and discrimination to your student affairs office who can take the necessary steps to protect you and other women in the future. Seek additional support and counseling if you need it. Remember that it is not your fault.

Pro tips

SEEKING SUPPORT

Most schools have women medical association chapters that provide support for women medical students. They can connect you with women role models and mentors.

RESOURCES

The samples and templates on the following pages will help guide you when making important decisions before, during, and after medical school. In some cases, you can write your entries directly on the pages. To make the best use of the templates, it is a good idea to copy them so that you can use them multiple times.

MEDICAL SCHOOL
COMPARISON CHART

School 1 Address: _____

Contact: _____

School 2 Address: _____

Contact: _____

School 3 Address: _____

Contact: _____

	School 1	School 2	School 3
GENERAL			
Name			
Location			
Tuition			
Financial aid			
Private vs public			
Class size			
Mission statement			
STATS			
USMLE pass rate			
Average USMLE score			
Residency match rate			
Average four-year graduation rate			
CURRICULUM			
Preclinical			
Grading policy			
Primary affiliated hospital ranking			
Affiliated clinical sites			
Patient population			

SCHOOL 1 NAME:

SERVICES

Well-being and mental health	
Academic support	
Advising and mentorship	
Other	

OPPORTUNITIES

Scholarly concentration program	
Student organizations of interest	
Joint degree programs	
Diversity, equity, and inclusion initiatives	
Volunteering opportunities	
Research	
Other	

INTANGIBLES

Impressions of students	
Impressions of faculty	
Impressions of administration	
Sense of fit	
Other	

Strengths	Weaknesses	Questions

SCHOOL 2 NAME:

SERVICES

Well-being and mental health	
Academic support	
Advising and mentorship	
Other	

OPPORTUNITIES

Scholarly concentration program	
Student organizations of interest	
Joint degree programs	
Diversity, equity, and inclusion initiatives	
Volunteering opportunities	
Research	
Other	

INTANGIBLES

Impressions of students	
Impressions of faculty	
Impressions of administration	
Sense of fit	
Other	

Strengths	Weaknesses	Questions

SCHOOL 3 NAME:

SERVICES

Well-being and mental health	
Academic support	
Advising and mentorship	
Other	

OPPORTUNITIES

Scholarly concentration program	
Student organizations of interest	
Joint degree programs	
Diversity, equity, and inclusion initiatives	
Volunteering opportunities	
Research	
Other	

INTANGIBLES

Impressions of students	
Impressions of faculty	
Impressions of administration	
Sense of fit	
Other	

Strengths	Weaknesses	Questions

BUDGET PLANNER
TEMPLATE

PERSONAL DETAILS

Student name

School/college

Date

MONTHLY INCOME

Item	Amount
Estimated monthly net income	
Financial aid award(s)	
Other income	
Total	$

DISCRETIONARY INCOME

Item	Amount
Monthly income	
Monthly expenses	
Semester expenses	
Difference	$

MONTHLY EXPENSES

Item	Amount
Rent	
Utilities	
Cell phone	
Groceries	
Auto expenses	
Student loans	
Other loans	
Credit cards	
Transportation	
Laundry	
Haircuts	
Medical expenses	
Entertainment	
Miscellaneous	
Total	$

SEMESTER EXPENSES

Item	Amount
Tuition	
Lab fees	
Other fees	
Books	
Deposits	
Insurance	
Total	$

STUDENT ORGANIZATIONS LOG

Name of organization

_____

Contact details

_____

Type of organization

_____

Meeting place

_____

Time of meeting

_____

Duration of membership

_____

Level of activity

_____

• Local

_____

• Regional

_____

• National

_____

Extent of involvement

_____

_____

What did I gain from the experience?

_____

_____

What did I contribute?

_____

_____

Useful contacts

1

_____

2

_____

3

_____

REASONS FOR JOINING

☐ Specialty exploration

☐ Leadership opportunity

☐ Research opportunity

☐ Practical skills opportunity

☐ Writing opportunity

☐ Networking

☐ Volunteer work

☐ Diverse membership

☐ Socializing

☐ Nonmedical emphasis

☐ Political emphasis

☐ Religious emphasis

☐ Sports emphasis

☐ Break from studying

☐ Resume booster

SMART GOALS TEMPLATE

S
Specific

Describe your goal

M
Measurable

How can you track your progress?

Attainable

Who is going to help you with your goals?

Who will be your accountability partner?

When will they check in with you?

R
Relevant

List the skills and resources you need in order to meet your goals

Time-Bound

Goal for check-in date 1	Goal for check-in date 2	Goal for check-in date 3
When?	When?	When?

YOUR LEADERSHIP SKILLS

SKILLS

Circle the number that reflects your skill level, where 1 is poor and 5 is excellent	At the start of medical school	At the start of clinical rotations	At the end of clinical rotations
PERSONAL QUALITIES AND EMOTIONAL INTELLIGENCE			
Self-awareness	1 2 3 4 5	1 2 3 4 5	1 2 3 4 5
Cultural sensitivity	1 2 3 4 5	1 2 3 4 5	1 2 3 4 5
Professionalism	1 2 3 4 5	1 2 3 4 5	1 2 3 4 5
Empathy	1 2 3 4 5	1 2 3 4 5	1 2 3 4 5
Continuing personal development	1 2 3 4 5	1 2 3 4 5	1 2 3 4 5
COMMUNICATION SKILLS	1 2 3 4 5	1 2 3 4 5	1 2 3 4 5
Listening	1 2 3 4 5	1 2 3 4 5	1 2 3 4 5
Clear articulation of ideas—spoken	1 2 3 4 5	1 2 3 4 5	1 2 3 4 5
Clear articulation of ideas—written	1 2 3 4 5	1 2 3 4 5	1 2 3 4 5
Influencing	1 2 3 4 5	1 2 3 4 5	1 2 3 4 5
MANAGERIAL SKILLS	1 2 3 4 5	1 2 3 4 5	1 2 3 4 5
Delegating	1 2 3 4 5	1 2 3 4 5	1 2 3 4 5
Conflict management	1 2 3 4 5	1 2 3 4 5	1 2 3 4 5
Negotiation	1 2 3 4 5	1 2 3 4 5	1 2 3 4 5
Organization	1 2 3 4 5	1 2 3 4 5	1 2 3 4 5
Time management	1 2 3 4 5	1 2 3 4 5	1 2 3 4 5
TEAMWORK	1 2 3 4 5	1 2 3 4 5	1 2 3 4 5
Visioning	1 2 3 4 5	1 2 3 4 5	1 2 3 4 5
Relationship-building	1 2 3 4 5	1 2 3 4 5	1 2 3 4 5
Facilitating group discussion	1 2 3 4 5	1 2 3 4 5	1 2 3 4 5
Goal-setting	1 2 3 4 5	1 2 3 4 5	1 2 3 4 5
Giving and receiving feedback	1 2 3 4 5	1 2 3 4 5	1 2 3 4 5

SHADOWING LOG

Preceptor

Name

Specialty

Contact details

Duration of shadowing

From

To

What do I want to achieve?

Preparations needed

Questions to ask preceptor

1

2

3

Follow-up questions for home research

1

2

3

Positive aspects of the experience

Negative aspects of the experience

Feedback from preceptor

Things to do differently next time

PERSONAL DEVELOPMENT PLAN

HOW AM I DOING?

ACADEMIC PERFORMANCE

Progress made this past semester:

Strengths:

Areas for improvement:

CLINICAL SKILLS

Progress made this past semester:

Strengths:

Areas for improvement:

WELL-BEING

Progress made this past semester:

Strengths:

Areas for improvement:

TEAMWORK AND PROFESSIONALISM

Progress made this past semester:

Strengths:

Areas for improvement:

Goal	Actions to achieve goal	Evidence of achieving goal	Start date	End date

CLERKSHIP JOURNAL TEMPLATE

Rotation dates:

Attendings:

What I liked:

What I didn't like:

Cases to remember:

1

2

3

4

5

Most meaningful moment:

Insights I gleaned about specialty choice:

1

2

3

STEP 2 CK STUDY TEMPLATE

	Pediatrics	Surgery	Obstetrics/ Gynecology	Psychiatry	Internal Medicine	Practice Test and Review	Rest
Time	**Monday**	**Tuesday**	**Wednesday**	**Thursday**	**Friday**	**Saturday**	**Sunday**
6:30 > 7:00	Exercise	Exercise	Exercise	Exercise	Exercise	Exercise	
7:00 > 7:30							
7:30 > 8:00	Breakfast	Breakfast	Breakfast	Breakfast	Breakfast	Breakfast	
8:00 > 8:30							
8:30 > 9:00							
9:00 > 9:30							
9:30 > 10:00							
10:00 > 10:30	Content review	Content review	Content review	Content review	Content review	Practice Test	
10:30 > 11:00							
11:00 > 11:30							
11:30 > 12:00							
12:00 > 12:30							
12:30 > 13:00							
13:00 > 13:30							
13:30 > 14:00	Lunch	Lunch	Lunch	Lunch	Lunch	Lunch	
14:00 > 14:30							
14:30 > 15:00							
15:00 > 15:30							
15:30 > 16:00							
16:00 > 16:30	Questions, active recall	Questions, active recall	Questions, active recall	Questions, active recall	Questions, active recall	Review incorrects	
16:30 > 17:00							
17:00 > 17:30							
17:30 > 18:00							
18:00 > 18:30							
18:30 > 19:00							
19:00 > 19:30	Dinner	Dinner	Dinner	Dinner	Dinner	Dinner	
19:30 > 20:00							
20:00 > 20:30	Flex time	Flex time	Flex time	Flex time	Flex time	Flex time	
20:30 > 21:00							

WHY DO YOU WANT A CAREER IN MEDICINE?

ABOUT YOU

What drives you?

What life experiences stand out to you?

Why are they important?

Why did you go to medical school?

Why is studying medicine important to you?

What do you hope to achieve?

YOUR INTERESTS

What subject matter is most fascinating to you?

What kind of environment do you prefer—fast-paced or leisurely?

Do you like to see a variety of things or the same thing, but with a view to perfecting it?

How much patient contact do you want?

What kind of relationships with patients are you looking for—minimal, long-term, somewhere in between?

What patient populations do you enjoy interacting with the most?

Do you crave breadth or depth of knowledge in your area of focus?

Do you prefer immediate results or long-term outcomes?

VALUES

What kind of lifestyle do you envision in your future career?

How much leisure time would you like?

How much does the prestige of a specialty matter to you?

How important is financial compensation to you?

What do you find most meaningful in a future career in medicine?

SKILLS

What skills do you want to use in your practice?

Are you a pro at organizing people and coordinating logistics?

Do you love working with your hands and want to do something procedural?

Do you love talking and connecting with people?

Do you love solving complicated problems?

NARROW IT DOWN

Mark the specialties that appeal most to you

- [ ] Psychiatry
- [ ] Pediatrics
- [ ] Neurology
- [ ] Internal medicine
- [ ] Physical medicine and rehabilitation
- [ ] Pathology
- [ ] Family medicine
- [ ] Radiation oncology
- [ ] Obstetrics/gynecology
- [ ] Anesthesiology
- [ ] General surgery
- [ ] Medicine pediatrics
- [ ] Interventional radiology
- [ ] Emergency medicine
- [ ] Diagnostic radiology
- [ ] Plastic surgery
- [ ] Neurosurgery
- [ ] Otolaryngology
- [ ] Cardiothoracic surgery
- [ ] Vascular surgery
- [ ] Orthopedic surgery
- [ ] Ophthalmology
- [ ] Dermatology
- [ ] Urology

INTERDISCIPLINARY TEAM MEMBERS

TEAM MEMBER	OVERVIEW	TRAINING
Physician assistant (PA)	Licensed to practice medicine and supervised by a physician. Supervision doesn't have to be direct.	Bachelor's degree, 24–26-month PA program with both classroom and clinical instruction. Most PA programs award master's degrees.
Physical therapist (PT)	Treats individuals with impairment in movement and performs activities of daily living. Prevents further disability, alleviates pain, and restores function.	Master's or doctoral level. Must graduate from accredited post-baccalaureate PT program to be eligible for national licensure exam.
Occupational therapist (OT)	Helps patients perform tasks for everyday living or working.	Master's or doctoral level. Must complete supervised clinical internships and pass national exam.
Registered nurse (RN)	Provides and coordinates patient care and performs patient education. Licensed by state.	Diploma program, 2-year associate degree and/or 4-year bachelor of science in nursing (BSN).
Licensed practical nurse (LPN)	Works under supervision of RN or physician. Licensed by state.	1 year at a community college or vocational school.
Nurse practitioner (NP)	Licensed independent practitioner who can be a primary and/or specialty provider.	RN with advanced academic and supervised clinical training. Most have master's and some doctoral degree.

Registered dietician (RD)	Food and nutrition expert.	Bachelor's degree, practical program, national examination.
Speech-language pathologist (SLP)	Evaluates, diagnoses, and treats language, speech, or swallowing difficulties.	Graduate degree (master's or doctoral) and clinical fellowship. National exam.
Respiratory therapist (RT)	Evaluates and treats respiratory issues or those who need breathing support via mechanical means.	Approved college program, national exam, licensed.
Pharmacist (PharmD)	Ensures the safe and effective use of medications. Supports clinicians in ordering medication and interactions, and provides patient medication, education, and counseling.	Doctor of Pharmacy following at least 2 years of undergrad and 4 years of pharmacy school. Advanced position (such as clinical pharmacy) requires additional training.
Doctor of podiatric medicine (DPM)	Provides medical and surgical treatments for a variety of foot conditions.	Bachelor's degree, 4-year podiatric medical school and hospital-based residency.
Social worker (SW)	Assesses a patient's social, emotional, environmental, financial, and support needs. Critical for discharge planning and coordinating social services.	Master's degree in social work (MSW).
Certified registered nurse anesthetist (CRNA)	Provides anesthetics in diverse practice settings. Can be main anesthesia provider. Supervision varies by state.	RN with master's degree and advanced training in anesthesia (24–36 months) and national certification exam.
Certified nurse midwife (CNM)	Provides prenatal care, labor and delivery, postpartum care, routine gynecology, and family planning.	RN with midwifery training. All with bachelor's, most with master's or higher. National certification exam.

FURTHER READING

GROWTH VERSUS FIXED MINDSET

Dweck, Carol S., PhD, *Mindset: The New Psychology of Success*, Ballantine Books, 2007.

IMPOSTOR SYNDROME

Young, Valerie, EdD, *The Secret Thoughts of Successful Women: Why Capable People Suffer from the Impostor Syndrome and How to Thrive in Spite of It*, Currency, 2011.

FINANCES

AAMC's FIRST (Financial Information, Resources, Services, and Tools) program, students-residents. students-residents.aamc.org/financial-aid/resources

LEARNING STRATEGIES

Oakley, Barbara, PhD, *Learning How to Learn: How to Succeed in School Without Spending All Your Time Studying*, TarcherPerigee, 2018.

Learning Scientists, learningscientists.org

Louisiana State University Center for Academic Success, lsu.edu/cas/earnbettergrades/tipsandtools/index.php

Success Types, John Pelley, MBA, PhD (cognitive maps), ttuhsc.edu/medicine/medical-education/success-types

TEAMWORK AND LEADERSHIP

Community Tool Box (Center for Community Health and Development at the University of Kansas), ctb.ku.edu/en/leadership-and-management

Levi, Daniel J., *Group Dynamics for Teams*, SAGE Publications, Inc, 2013.

RESEARCH

International Committee of Medical Journal Editors (roles of authors and contributors), icmje.org/recommendations/browse/roles-and-responsibilities/defining-the-role-of-authors-and-contributors.html

WELL-BEING AND RESILIENCE

American Psychiatric Association (Resilience), apa.org/topics/resilience

Mindful, mindful.org

National Sleep Foundation, sleepfoundation.org

Psychology Today (Mindfulness), psychologytoday.com/us/basics/mindfulness

Substance Abuse and Mental Health Services Administration, U.S. Department of Health & Human Services (8 Dimensions of Wellness), samhsa.gov

YouTube: Cultivating Resilience | Greg Eells | TEDxCortland (January 16, 2015)

MAINTAINING RELATIONSHIPS

Bonior, Andrea, PhD, *The Friendship Fix*,
St. Martin's Griffin, 2011.

Chretien, Katherine, MD (Ed), *Mothers in
Medicine: Career, Practice, and Life Lessons
Learned*, Springer, 2018.

CHOOSING A SPECIALTY

AAMC Careers in Medicine, www.aamc.org/cim

Freeman, Brian, *The Ultimate Guide to Choosing a
Medical Specialty*, McGraw-Hill Education, 2018.

PROFESSIONAL IDENTITY

Levinson, Wendy, Shiphra Ginsburg, Fred Hafferty, and
Catherine Lucy, *Understanding Medical Professionalism*,
McGraw-Hill Education Foundation, 2014.

Pho, Kevin, MD and Susan Gay, *Establishing,
Managing, and Protecting Your Online Reputation:
A Social Media Guide for Physicians and Medical
Practices*, Greenbranch Publishing, 2013.

DIVERSITY, EQUITY, AND INCLUSION

Georgetown University School of Medicine's
Stop, Talk, Roll, som.georgetown.edu/
diversityandinclusion/studentorganizations/
stoptalkroll

Guide to Allyship, guidetoallyship.com

Project Implicit (Implicit Association Test),
implicit.harvard.edu/implicit/takeatest.html

GLOSSARY

Advocacy The act of supporting a specific cause, issue, or group of people. The term "advocate" comes from the Latin term *advocare*, which means to "add" a "voice."

Ally A person who proactively contributes to an inclusive environment and stands up for people who are marginalized.

Altruistic Being mindful of others; having regard for the well-being or best interests of others; opposed to egotism.

Alumnus/alumna (pl. alumni) A former student of an educational institution. Most colleges or universities have alumni organizations whose members are engaged in various school-related activities.

Attending A physician (MD or DO) who has completed residency and serves as a supervising physician to medical students and residents.

Bias The preference of one thing over another. It can be either positive or negative. In relationships, however, any tendency to believe that certain social groups are better than others can result in some people being treated unfairly.

Boards/board exams Standardized exams that are required for medical licensure; passing these exams is often part of medical school graduation requirements.

Burnout A state of emotional exhaustion, cynicism, and reduced sense of personal accomplishment as a result of chronic professional stress.

Clerkship Required clinical rotation in a major discipline such as family medicine, internal medicine, obstetrics/gynecology, pediatrics, psychiatry, or surgery.

Clinical Pertaining, or related, to the direct observation of a patient; also a reference to the last two years of medical school when students rotate across various medical specialties in the hospital or clinic setting.

Clinical research Research related to patients, such as chart reviews, observational studies, and clinical trials, as opposed to laboratory-based research.

Clinical rotation An immersive hospital or clinic experience in a specific medical discipline that is either elective (of the student's choosing) or mandatory (*see also*, "clerkship").

Cognitive diversity The inclusion of various unique attitudes, perspectives, or learning styles in a work environment; a quality that improves a team's pursuit of a common goal.

Cohort Members of a similar group of people (such as students) who begin an educational program together, often take some courses together, and graduate in the same term and year.

Community service Participation in events within the school or community that befit a charitable or altruistic cause.

Concept map A diagram that visually represents relationships between concepts; a form of active learning.

Curriculum A set of requirements that serves to guide and standardize an educational experience.

Dean The top or executive leader of a specific area of a college, university, or private school; has primary management and leadership responsibility for their unit.

Depersonalization The act of feeling separate or detached from one's job; can occur as a consequence of burnout.

Digital footprint A person's traceable record of online activity, including social media posts, browsing/communication history, and more, that can be used by colleagues and future employers to assess overall character and values.

Diversity The inclusion of varied beliefs, practices, experiences, and/or ways of life, including, but not limited to, age, gender, race, ethnicity, language, sexual orientation, religion, marital status, and socioeconomic status.

Dual-apply The act of applying to more than one medical specialty for residency.

Elective(s) Optional courses that students may select from a list of alternatives, that are designed to enhance the students' primary educational program.

Emotional intelligence The ability to identify, manage, and regulate one's own emotions, and those of others, for effective interpersonal interactions; facilitates communication, empathy, and conflict management; a valued leadership skill.

Equity Due effort to recognize, address, and eliminate systemic societal barriers for historically underrepresented groups by providing all with appropriate means for advancement; an important ideal that mandates equal opportunities for all.

Ethics A philosophy or internal belief system concerned with differentiating what is morally right versus what is morally wrong.

Extracurricular An activity outside of academic schoolwork that a student chooses to participate in.

Faculty Appointed staff at a university that often have a clinical, teaching, research, or administrative role.

Feedback sandwich A method for delivering feedback, first starting with a positive point of feedback, next giving constructive criticism, then ending with another positive point.

Fellowship Subspecialty training that follows residency.

Flex time An allotted time, integrated into one's schedule, to allow for personal/wellness needs or any delays/setbacks in productivity.

Hidden curriculum The unspoken, unintended lessons and values that students are exposed to while being in the learning environment that may lie in contrast to those formally taught during medical school.

Honor code A formal document outlining expectations for professional and just behavior throughout medical school, often signed by medical students during the White Coat Ceremony.

Implicit bias Also known as "unconscious bias"; stereotypes and associations that people have about groups of people that they are not consciously aware of and may contradict their espoused values.

Impostor syndrome The persistent inability to believe that one's success is deserved or has been legitimately achieved as a result of one's own efforts or skills.

Inclusivity Intentional joining of historically excluded or underrepresented groups into shared decision-making, activities, and proposals that promote and perpetuate opportunities for all.

Intern A person who has graduated from medical school and is in their first year of residency.

Mentee A student who is trained or counseled by a mentor. Though the mentor is the more senior in relation to experience, the mentee is also responsible for contributing to the relationship through consistent communication and feedback.

Mentor A person who has expertise in a specific field, who serves as a role model and trusted source of information and guidance for a mentee.

Metacognition An awareness and understanding of one's own thought processes.

Microaggression A seemingly subtle, sometimes inadvertent gibe, typically toward a marginalized individual, that can accumulate over time to lead to increased stress and perpetuate discrimination.

Mind break A break from focused cognitive work, such as studying or problem-solving, in order for the brain to switch to diffuse mode thinking.

Mindfulness The act of being fully aware and present in the moment in a nonjudgmental way.

Oral presentation A structured way to communicate patient information to others on the health care team.

Organization fair An opportunity for medical students, usually shortly after orientation, to learn about/sign up for student groups on campus.

Personal statement A personal narrative or essay that reflects a medical student's interests, experiences, and fit with their intended specialty, submitted as part of their residency application.

Plagiarism The act of submitting another person's ideas or words as one's own or without detailed use of citations or proper attribution.

Preceptor In shadowing, a doctor or other experienced practitioner who supervises and teaches clinical medicine.

Preclinical Typically the first 1½ to 2 years of medical school spent in classroom-based and laboratory-based learning; the time period in medical school prior to the start of clinical rotations.

Premedical The time period prior to medical school, typically in college, spent in preparation and in anticipation of entering medical school.

Registrar The registrar (and associated office) at a medical school is responsible for student registration and enrollment, management of all student records, verification and processing of attendance, transcript requests, and monitoring satisfactory progress to graduation.

Remediation A process that allows students who fail particular requirements of a course to remedy the failures and meet course expectations.

Residency A clinical training period, generally ranging from three to seven years, that starts after medical school to prepare physicians to practice in their specific specialty.

Scholarly concentration A program offered at some schools, where students perform research with faculty mentors and develop expertise in a specific area of study to complement the medical school curriculum.

Scholarship Financial award that may be applied to medical school tuition or other related expenses.

Shadow To observe a doctor's or other experienced practitioner's patient–physician encounters in order to gain a better understanding of clinical medicine.

Social justice Equal access to opportunities, wealth, health, and privileges within a society; often linked to advocacy for marginalized populations.

Specialty A branch of medical practice, such as pediatrics, psychiatry, or general surgery; medical students choose a specialty in which to practice and complete a residency in that specialty.

Stipend A regular sum of money paid for services or to defray expenses.

Transcript A record of courses taken and grades received from an institution of study.

Tutor Someone who provides academic assistance or instruction to a learner.

Upstander Someone who observes a person being the recipient of bias, discrimination, or harassment and intervenes in support; the opposite of a bystander.

INDEX

ACKNOWLEDGMENTS

AUTHOR ACKNOWLEDGMENTS

Thank you to all the students, residents, and colleagues who contributed their thoughts and words of wisdom to this book, in the name of helping future students. Students: Olivia Silva, Sangrag Garg, Meera Krishnamoorthy, Soujanya Kondameedi, Christopher Weston, Brittney Gordon, Rose Milando, Harleen Marwah, Koumudi Thingaru, Paulina Ong, Daniel Bestorous, Ramin Garmany, Zayna Bakizada, Laura Upton, Garrett Berger, Taylor Wahrenbrock, Eleanor Gerhard, Tomi Ifelayo, Reem Al Shabeeb, Chantal Nguyen. Residents: Maria Henry, Bernard Mendis, Michelle Chen, Christian Hendrix, Max Mandelbaum. Colleagues: Erica Levine, Andrew Olson, Marcy Verduin, Kimberly Tartaglia, Meredith Schor, Jeffrey Hanson, John Pelley, Ellen Goldman, Rajesh Mangrulkar, Rachel Wolfson, Lisa Willett, Thomas Koenig, Wei Wei Lee, Vineet Arora, Avital O'Glasser, Kerry-Ann Mitchell, Liselotte Dyrbye, Cynthia Powell, Karen Hauer, Adam Killian, Ria Roberts, Susan Cheng, Paul Aronowitz, Grace Henry, Yolanda Haywood, Rhonda Goldberg, Richard Simons.

Thank you to all of my students, past and present, who inspire me daily.

Special thanks to: Terry Kind for her friendship, peer mentorship, and support; Tony Artino for his generous wisdom regarding all things learning and research-related; Hilit Mechaber for her inspiration and mentorship; Lorenzo Norris for always being there as a colleague; and most of all to my husband Jean-Paul and our children Jolie, Jean-Luc, and Pascal for all of their love and support.

The publisher acknowledges the following, whose work forms the basis of infographics that feature in this book: John Pelley, MPA, PhD, for the Concept Maps on page 47; the Substance Abuse Mental Health Services Administration, U.S. Department of Health and Human Services for the Eight Dimensions of Wellness on page 122; and S. M. Cheng's "Stop, Talk, Roll: How to Deal with Tough Communication Exchanges in the Medical Workplace," (2017, May 10). Retrieved from https://som.georgetown.edu/diversityandinclusion/studentorganizations/stoptalkroll/, for Responding to Microaggressions and Discrimination on pages 194–195.

IMAGE CREDITS